CHYTRAEUS

On Sacrifice

A REFORMATION TREATISE IN BIBLICAL THEOLOGY

David Chytraeus' "De Sacrificiis" of 1569
Translated for the First Time into a
Modern Language and Edited in Translation

by

JOHN WARWICK MONTGOMERY

M. A., S. T. M., Ph. D.
Chairman, Department of History
Waterloo Lutheran University
Waterloo, Ontario

1962

CONCORDIA PUBLISHING HOUSE
Saint Louis, Missouri

Concordia Publishing House, Saint Louis, Missouri 63118
Copyright 1962 by Concordia Publishing House

ISBN 0-570-03747-6
Library of Congress Catalog Card No. 61-18224

CONTENTS

* *Section headings have been supplied by the editor on the basis of the natural organization of material in the text.*

For

THE REV. IRVING C. HOFFMAN, B. A., B. D.
Missionary in Algeria under the North Africa Mission
οὗ οὐκ ἔστιν ἄξιος ὁ κόσμος

INTRODUCTION

The name David Chytraeus will mean little to many who take the present work in hand. This may well appear surprising when one realizes that this man, who studied under Luther and Melanchthon, is considered "the last of the fathers of the Lutheran Church"; that he was one of the three individuals chiefly responsible for that great Lutheran confessional document, the Formula of Concord, and in fact served virtually as personal author of its most historically significant articles — those dealing with free will and the Lord's Supper; and that his theological productions were so many in number that the British Museum's latest *General Catalogue of Printed Books* devotes over five columns (eighty-seven entries) to him, the *Catalogue général des livres imprimés* of the Bibliothèque Nationale in Paris lists under his name forty-seven works, covering more than six printed columns, and as of March 1960 he is represented by over one hundred and twenty cards in the National Union Catalog at the Library of Congress in Washington, D. C.[1]

Even more remarkable, perhaps, is the contrast between David Chytraeus' reputation today and that in his own time. His biographer Schütz notes that "it almost exceeds belief" that, while Chytraeus was still living, two great collected editions of his exegetical works were published in folio within a ten-year period — "when similar editions of the major works of other Lutheran theologians were scarcely issued at all."[2] And the historian of the University of Rostock states unqualifiedly that Chytraeus' contributions in the scholarly, ecclesiastical, and political spheres were matched only by his influence at Rostock — and that he must be

[1] The count was made and forwarded to me by George A. Schwegmann, Jr., Chief, Union Catalog Division, Library of Congress (letter dated 3-10-60).

[2] O. F. Schütz, *De Vita Davidis Chytraei* (Hamburg, 1720—28), III, 420. Schütz attempts to explain the amazing fact of the two editions on the basis of the poor printing job done on the first edition, but this of course merely begs the question; had Chytraeus not been very popular, would a second publisher have taken a chance on a second edition of his works regardless of the condition of the first edition?

considered the "creator and sustainer" of the "imperishable glory" which the university achieved in the second half of the sixteenth century.[3]

Why, over against these impressive facts, is David Chytraeus a member of the vast body of forgotten theologians? It appears that there are at least two reasons — the second being considerably more important than the first. Latin was the language of theological scholarship during Chytraeus' time, and thus it was his scholarly language. But Latin had ceased to function as the general medium of academic communication by the end of the eighteenth century. All Latin writers, for this reason, have had an uphill fight for recognition during the last century and a half. They have required editors and translators to reintroduce them to the scholarly public — a public experiencing a far different *Zeitgeist* from their own.[4] And the more prolix or difficult the author's Latin style, the less the chance that an interpreter will appear in his behalf. For Chytraeus, then, whose exegetical labors were performed entirely in the Latin tongue and in a style which even his contemporaries considered involved, it is not so strange that fame ceased about 1750 — that point which more than a few historians have considered as the "great divide" in the history of Western culture.

But others have survived this dividing line; why not Chytraeus? A theologian's reputation is particularly bound up with the ideological climate succeeding his own. Also in this respect Chytraeus has been at a disadvantage. At the time of his death, in the year ushering in the seventeenth century, Lutheran (and indeed all Protestant) theology was rapidly moving in the direction of great systematic, dogmatic productions. Chytraeus, however, like the principal reformers who were his teachers, was an exegete — a Biblical theologian — by interest and temperament, not a systematician. The prime movers of the Reformation, such as Luther, easily weathered the period of "Orthodoxy" on the basis of their historical importance, but one such as Chytraeus, who neither introduced a Refor-

3 Otto Krabbe, *Die Universität Rostock im fünfzehnten und sechzehnten Jahrhundert,* I (Rostock, 1854), 550. See also this author's *Aus dem kirchlichen und wissenschaftlichen Leben Rostocks* (Berlin, 1863), pp. 20 ff.; and his *David Chytraeus* (Rostock, 1870).

4 In his J. H. Gray lectures, H. W. Garrod makes such acts of reintroduction the defining mark of scholarship (*Scholarship: Its Meaning and Value* [Cambridge: Cambridge University Press, 1946]).

mation nor produced a *Loci theologici,* was almost inevitably shifted from the center to the periphery of theological interest.

And Chytraeus suffered from the seventeenth-century dogmaticians in still another way. When these systematicians themselves began to diminish in reputation, they carried Chytraeus with them. The fact that he had been associated with Chemnitz in the drafting of the Formula of Concord reduced his worth in the eyes of those who came to look on such confessional statements as manifesting unfortunate proclivities. In a word, Chytraeus received the damning appellation of "orthodox Lutheran theologian." The downhill slide to obscurity then became a foregone conclusion. For Pietism, which mushroomed from the humble beginnings made by Spener and Francke, tended to see in the works of the "Orthodoxists" a definite deterrent to personal, heart religion; and the so-called Enlightenment, which followed hard on the heels of Pietism, viewed the doctrinal products of the sixteenth and seventeenth centuries as almost beneath contempt. Nineteenth-century Romanticism (as its name suggests) found little of a congenial nature in the Aristotelian-scholastic labors of the fathers of the Lutheran Church. The religious liberalism of our own century, with its roots sunk deep into the soil of eighteenth-century rationalism, has likewise been prone to overlook the work of those in former times who by its standards were hopelessly bigoted and opinionated. To many Americans especially — with their fetish of "religious toleration" (sometimes indistinguishable from religious indifference) — the Formula of Concord and its authors breathe a heavy, unpleasant, foreign atmosphere — one which they would prefer to avoid.

The last several decades, however, have seen both the rise of a strong Biblical theology movement and a great increase in Reformation scholarship and research. Taken together, these revived interests may well find something of value in a basic work by Chytraeus hitherto unavailable in any language but Latin,[5] and one which because of its subject matter (Biblical sacrifice) closely relates

---

[5] Only two of Chytraeus' works seem ever to have appeared in English — and one of these is but an extract. They are: (1) *A Postil, or orderly disposing of certeine Epistles usually red in the Church of God, uppon the Sundayes, and Holydays throughout the whole yeere,* trans. Arthur Golding (London, 1570; another ed., ibid., 1577). (2) *A Soveraigne Salve for a Sick Soule,* trans. W. F. (London, 1590). Copies of these works are in the British Museum and are widely available on microfilm in this country

to the author's main contribution to the Formula of Concord (Article VII, on the Lord's Supper). It is hoped, in short, that the καιρός has now arrived when such a translation and edition as this can drive home the truth of Schmauk and Benze's magnificent assertion: "We doubt whether the Lutheran Church has ever had a body of men greater in learning and piety than those who elaborated the Formula of Concord. Although they were human, and their faults were open and known, as were those of the three chief apostles of our Lord, yet the honesty of their purpose, the depth of their piety, and the sincerity of their conviction cause their life to add to, instead of detracting from, the validity of the Confession." [6]

The Life of Chytraeus [7]

David Chytraeus (Grecization of Kochhafe) was born on February 26, 1531,[8] in the small town of Ingelfingen, Württemberg.

because they appear in Pollard and Redgrave's Short-Title Catalogue (S. T. C. 5263—5265; University microfilms nos. 11774 and 11776). The second item is extracted from Chytraeus' Regulae vitae. Note that both translations were issued during the author's own lifetime.

[6] T. E. Schmauk and C. T. Benze, The Confessional Principle and the Confessions of the Lutheran Church (Philadelphia: General Council Publication Board, 1911), p. 726.

[7] The following biographical sketch derives from these basic sources: Schütz, Vita (the four-volume comprehensive biography, incorporating material from Chytraeus' correspondence, unpublished sources, etc.); and Melchior Adam, "David Chytraeus," in his Vitae Germanorum theologicorum (Heidelberg, 1620 [also Frankfurt, 1653; etc.]), pp. 681—696 (based on the funeral orations for Chytraeus delivered in 1600 by Johann Goldstein and Christoph Sturz). Of collateral value have been Theodor Pressel, David Chyträus (Elberfeld, 1862 [in Leben und ausgewählte Schriften der Väter und Begründer der lutherischen Kirche, VIII]); Krabbe, opera cit.; "David Chyträus," in the Allgemeine deutsche Biographie, ed. by the Historische Commission bei der K. Akademie der Wissenschaften (Leipzig, 1875 to 1912), IV, 254—256; Georg Loesche, "Chytraeus, David," in Realencyklopädie für protestantische Theologie und Kirche, founded by J. J. Herzog, 3d ed. by Albert Hauck (Leipzig, 1896—1913), IV, 112—116, and XXIII, 310, hereafter cited as PRE (this article appears in a somewhat condensed form in The New Schaff-Herzog Encyclopedia of Religious Knowledge [New York: Funk and Wagnalls, 1908—12], III, 116, 117). Note also the appropriate entries in Karl Schottenloher, Bibliographie zur deutschen Geschichte im Zeitalter der Glaubensspaltung 1517—1585 (Leipzig, 1936—40).

[8] The date sometimes appears as February 26, 1530, rather than 1531;

His father, Matthew Kochhafe, was Lutheran pastor for the village, which is located on the Kocher River, 43 miles northeast of Stuttgart and 14 miles southwest of Mergentheim; in 1952 its population was only 1,812.

David became a student at the University of Tübingen at a very young age — apparently at the age of nine. He first studied law, then philology and philosophy, and finally turned to the queen of the sciences, theology. The theological influences under which he came at Tübingen were powerful ones — including Prof. Joachim Camerarius (1500—1574), the biographer of Melanchthon and his assistant in preparing the Apology of the Augsburg Confession; Prof. Erhard Schnepf (1495—1558), who later helped to organize the University of Jena; and Deacon Jakob Heerbrand (1521 to 1600), the author of a *Compend of Theology* which was so widely used that it was even translated into Greek. Camerarius was a Philippist who later favored the Leipzig Interim, whereas Heerbrand and Schnepf were deposed from their positions at Tübingen in 1548 because of their orthodox Lutheran opposition to the Interim. It is inconceivable that such influential minds as these should not have left a permanent impression on the young scholar; and it is significant in this connection that Schmauk summarizes his entire career with the words, "Chytraeus was of the manner and heart of Melanchthon, with the doctrine of Luther." [9]

For several years, therefore, Chytraeus learned of Luther and Melanchthon secondhand; it was thus quite natural that once he had received his baccalaureate and his master's degree (both when he was fifteen), he should have proceeded to Wittenberg to study at the feet of the "old man" and his irenic colleague. He was invited to live in Melanchthon's house (probably through the influence of Camerarius) and became one of Melanchthon's favorite pupils. For a few short weeks, or possibly months, he heard Dr. Luther himself lecture on Genesis — a lectureship which Luther had begun ten years before (1535) and which he continued right up to the time of his last journey to Eisleben, early in 1546. Chytraeus also attended the lectures of Paul Eber (1511—1569),

prior to the Gregorian calendar reform (1582, but not accepted in Germany until about 1700 and in England until 1751), March 25, not January 1, marked the beginning of the new year.

[9] Schmauk, p. xxi.

11

who had been appointed professor of Latin at Wittenberg only shortly before this (in 1544). Eber, like Camerarius, was later to show himself as a thoroughgoing Philippist.[10] It is reasonable to suppose that at Wittenberg Chytraeus determined that he would never willingly depart from the clear-cut, evangelical, and thoroughly Biblical theology of Father Luther; yet on the other hand his friendship for Melanchthon was such that throughout his life, in the words of Schmauk, he "would never breathe a word against his beloved Melanchthon."[11]

Chytraeus' stay at Wittenberg was a brief one, however, because of the Schmalkald War. In the latter part of 1546 he went to Heidelberg, where he taught languages. In the summer of 1547 war conditions brought him again to his alma mater (Tübingen); and at the beginning of 1548 he returned to Wittenberg, where, on Melanchthon's advice, he began to lecture on rhetoric, astronomy, and the latter's *Loci communes*. Chytraeus' astronomical studies "are reflected in the subsequent viewpoint of Tycho Brahe," his younger contemporary.[12]

About 1550 Chytraeus visited Switzerland, Italy, etc.; and on his return home in 1551 a pleasant surprise awaited him. Dukes Heinrich V ("the Peaceable") and Johann Albrecht I of Mecklenburg[13] presented him with an invitation to the University of Rostock. He accepted and early in the same year accompanied his friend Johann Aurifaber[14] to this historic city, which was to

[10] Philip Schaff, *Creeds of Christendom,* 4th ed. (New York: Harper, 1877), I, 267.

[11] Op. cit., p. 560.

[12] Loesche in *PRE.* Many Lutheran theologians at this time were interested in astronomical-astrological studies; see Schütz, *Vita,* I, 45—47. My thanks to Professor Jaroslav Pelikan of Yale University for bringing this astrological point to my attention in personal conversation.

[13] Johann Albrecht (1525—1576) was the nephew of Duke Heinrich (1479—1552). For excellent biographical sketches of these two men, see the *Allgemeine deutsche Biographie,* XI, 542, 543; and XIV, 239, 243.

[14] Aurifaber (1517—1568) should not be confused with his more famous contemporary of the same name, Johann Aurifaber (1519—1575), who witnessed Luther's death and was coeditor of the Jena edition of Luther's works and his *Tabletalk.* Chytraeus' friend, who became professor at Rostock, was the chief author of the Mecklenburg *Kirchenordnung* (1551—52; Chytraeus assisted him in preparing it) and later served as professor at Koenigsberg and still later as pastor at Breslau, where he died.

become his permanent home. The Baltic port of Rostock (100 miles northeast of Hamburg), founded in 1189 on the site of an ancient Wendish stronghold, had been one of the most powerful members of the Hanseatic League and boasted a 13th-century church (St. Mary's) and a university founded in 1419.[15] Because of his youth, Chytraeus began his teaching in the academy *(Pädagogium)* rather than in the university proper. On April 21, 1551, he delivered his first lectures on basic Christian doctrine and on the works of Herodotus.

In 1553 he began to lecture in his field of special interest — theology proper. He delivered lectures on the Old and the New Testament — both "encyclopedic" lectures (including what today would be covered by general survey, hermeneutics, and Biblical introduction courses) and lectures of an exegetical character.[16] On November 12 of the same year he married one Margarete Smedes, who bore him seven children, only two of whom (both daughters) reached adulthood.[17]

Fifteen fifty-five was a particularly important year in his life. It marked the publication of his celebrated *Regulae vitae,* which "began his far-reaching theological productivity."[18] Also in that

---

[15] About twenty percent of the city was destroyed in World War II, including St. Mary's Church and a large part of the holdings of the university library.

[16] It is significant that from the outset of his teaching career Chytraeus lectured with a view toward the publication of his material in permanent form. Out of his academy teaching came three significant books: (1) *Catechesis* (Wittenberg, 1555 and after), an "able work, used for almost a century in universities, gymnasia, and public schools" (Loesche); (2) *Chronologia historiae Herodoti et Thucydidis* (Strassburg, 1563, etc.); (3) *De lectione historiarum recte instituenda* (Rostock, 1563, etc.), a work "important for the history of historiography" (Loesche).

[17] A famous Latin poet, Johann Stigel (1515—1562; see the *Allgemeine deutsche Biographie,* XXXVI, 228—230) wrote a lengthy epithalamium for Chytraeus' marriage. It is titled "In nuptias Davidis Chytraei" and is printed in the *Delitiae poetarum Germanorum huius superiorisque aevi illustrium,* ed. Jan Gruter, VI (Frankfurt, 1612), 473—483. For numerous "epitaphia liberorum aliquot Davidis Chytraei ab amicis scripta," see the unpaginated appendix to Pt. I of Chytraeus' *De morte et vita aeterna* (Wittenberg, 1581—82).

[18] *Allgemeine deutsche Biographie.* See above, note 5. Loesche, however, calls the work "colorless"; his overall view of Chytraeus is clearly on the

year he attended the highly important Diet of Augsburg [19] — the first of many such conferences which he would attend during his long lifetime. He was offered the position of university superintendent at Rostock, but he declined; nevertheless "he was looked upon as the pillar of the institution." [20]

In 1557 Chytraeus took part in the extremely disappointing Consultation of Worms. This conference was completely unsuccessful in reconciling Lutheran and Roman Catholic theologians because (1) the Romanists refused to accept the Bible as the only and final norm of doctrine, and (2) the evangelicals presented a divided front — with the Flacians opposing the Wittenbergers. It may well be that at the consultation Chytraeus first saw the absolute necessity of securing a consistent, unequivocal Lutheran doctrinal stand; for the very next year, in the name of the Mecklenburg theologians assembled at Wismar, he composed a declaration opposing the Frankfort Recess.[21] This action on his part marked the beginning of personal labors which culminated in Articles II and VII of the Formula of Concord, an aspect of Chytraeus' life to which a separate section will be devoted below.

negative side (he speaks of his exegetical works as "glossatory, dogmatizing commentaries of slight importance"). In all probability Loesche was influenced by Calvinist or broad-church sentiments. He makes the misleading statement that Chytraeus "found the forms of the true doctrines 'mediocriter constituta' in the Formula of Concord" — the point being, not (as Loesche implies) that Chytraeus objected to the orthodoxy of the Formula (he himself wrote a good part of it!) but that he would have preferred its doctrinal discussions to be more extensive (see below).

[19] It was of course at this Diet that the Religious Peace of Augsburg was established; the Diet was the crowning blow to Charles V — shortly after this he retired to Spain, where he died in 1558 (see Karl Brandi, *Emperor Charles V,* trans. C. V. Wedgwood [New York, 1939]).

[20] Loesche, in *PRE.* He later served several terms as rector of the university.

[21] "In March, 1558, some of the nobility attended the coronation of Emperor Ferdinand at Frankfort. There they conferred on the problem of unity. At their direction Melanchthon wrote a union document called the Frankfort Recess, which was subscribed by the leading princes. They agreed to censor all teaching and books on the basis of this document. But Melanchthon's phrases were so ambiguous that even Calvin said he could accept them. As a result other Lutheran princes rejected the document and the disunity continued." (Allbeck, *Studies in the Lutheran Confessions* [Philadelphia: Muhlenberg, 1952], p. 245)

Chytraeus became regular professor of theology at Rostock in 1561 and on April 29 of that year was elevated to the doctorate. The promotion of the interests of the university lay close to his heart; he labored for the completion of the (university) *Formula concordiae* and drew up the statutes of the theological faculty.

In 1566 Chytraeus accompanied the duke to the *Reichstag* in Augsburg. He was gradually becoming known far beyond the borders of Mecklenburg — not only for his scholarship but especially for his moderate, intelligent organizing ability.

In 1568, when Emperor Maximilian II granted free exercise of religion on the basis of the Augsburg Confession to the Lutheran estates in Lower and Upper Austria, it was not strange that these estates included Chytraeus on the commission to draw up the required *Kirchenordnung*. Early in 1569 he arrived in Austria to begin a grueling fourfold task: the preparation of a liturgy, an order for superintendents and consistories, an *examen ordinandorum*, and an exposition of the Augsburg Confession. The Flacian ministers made the fourth job a hard one, but finally it was accomplished. Chytraeus returned home, having received the praise of the emperor. The subsequent publication of the liturgy (in 1571) was unfortunately accompanied by bitter controversy, which had to be dealt with by force.

In 1569 Chytraeus published one of the very few polemic works of his entire career: a judgment against Johann Beatus (Saliger, Seliger), whose deviationist views on the Lord's Supper had caused him to lose his pastoral charge in Lübeck and who had thereupon come to Rostock and was proceeding to preach the same doctrines from the pulpit of St. Mary's. As a result of Chytraeus' statement, Beatus was forced to leave Rostock as well.[22] In the statement which he wrote, Chytraeus promoted the establishment

[22] Important factors in Saliger's removal were his Flacian anthropology and his refractory character. The most comprehensive and generally available reference on the subject is J. Wiggers, "Der Saligersche Abendmahlstreit in der zweiten Hälfte des 16. Jahrhunderts," *Zeitschrift für die historische Theologie,* XVIII (1848), 613—666; however, it should be noted that this article suffers somewhat from defective interpretation of the data. Saliger stirred up great doctrinal controversy and commotion almost everywhere he went, and his influence was still felt in Rostock at the end of the century.

of a Rostock consistory. He himself was appointed to its first ecclesiastical council (June 22, 1570).[23]

Chytraeus' fortieth year was saddened by the death, on April 18, 1571, of Margarete, the wife of his youth. That same year he first published his great work in the area of historical dogmatics, *The History of the Augsburg Confession* (German ed., Rostock, 1576 et al; Latin ed., Frankfort, 1578).[24] Shortly afterwards he felt compelled to defend the work against Joachim II's court preacher Georg Coelestin, an "ambitious" man of "possible duplicity."[25]

The following year (on February 19, 1572) Chytraeus married again. Interestingly, his second wife was also named Margarete (Margarete Pegel). There were two surviving children of this marriage; their names were Ulrich and David, Jr.

Because of Chytraeus' organizational activity in Austria, the estates of Styria had their attention drawn to him. In September 1573 they invited him to reorder their church affairs (following the confirmation by Archduke Charles of the religious compromise to be effected there). On January 2, 1574, he arrived at Graz, the capital of Styria (located eighty miles southwest of Vienna), and managed to complete the *Kirchenordnung* by May of the same year.

[23] He had not drawn up the Consistorial Order but merely examined and approved it after his return from Austria.

[24] Schmauk gives (in English translation) numerous extended quotations from this work in his *Confessional Principle* (see especially pp. 291, 305). These quotations reveal quite well both the deep piety and the sound common sense which Chytraeus possessed. Chytraeus' *History of the Augsburg Confession* receives mention in James Westfall Thompson's *A History of Historical Writing*, I (New York: Macmillan, 1942), 528. Zeeden's negative evaluation is based on a Roman Catholic confessional opposition to the Reformation: "A truly mediaeval naïveté was the mark of [a] pragmatic attempt to recognize the finger of God in each single event of the Reformation. David Chyträus believed that the Emperor Charles V became involved in his French wars between 1521 and 1529 'through a special provision of God,' so that in his absence the Edict of Worms could be carried through unhindered 'and the doctrine of the Gospel be planted and spread more surely and more widely in Germany and other lands.'" Ernst Walter Zeeden, *The Legacy of Luther: Martin Luther and the Reformation in the Estimation of the German Lutherans from Luther's Death to the Beginning of the Age of Goethe,* trans. Ruth Mary Bethell (London: Hollis & Carter, 1954), p. 30.

[25] Schmauk, pp. 535, 560.

He received a vote of thanks and returned home to take up his relations with the Scandinavian kingdoms.[26]

In 1576 Chytraeus assisted Duke Julius of Brunswick in the establishment of the University of Helmstedt. Though not in existence today, this institution was a real academic power in the seventeenth century. Connected with it was the famous Wolfenbüttel Library, of which Leibniz was for a time the librarian.[27]

Chytraeus made his single serious historical blunder in 1576 — though the error was not of the magnitude some have supposed. He published what he describes in his own words as "really and truly the right and genuine first copy of the [Augsburg] Confession, as it reads word by word, which was delivered to his Imperial Majesty at the Diet in 1530."[28] This German copy of the Confession was the supposed original which had been "rediscovered" at Mainz and presented in 1566 to Georg Coelestin[29] and Andreas Zoch (the counselor of the Archbishop of Magdeburg) when they sought the genuine text for Elector Joachim II. In 1572 this text was received into the *Corpus doctrinae Brandenburgicum* as authentic, and it was eventually made the basis of the German text of the Book of Concord. Actually the Mainz original permanently disappeared sometime between 1540 and 1545, and the text presented to Coelestin and Zoch, and printed by Chytraeus, was "the copy of a poor copy."[30] However, it should be clearly understood that this copy was *not* a Variata, and its textual errors, though

---

[26] That Chytraeus' influence was strong in the Scandinavian lands is quite clear from the title of the polemic written against him by the contemporary Jesuit Antonius Possevinus: *Adversus Davidis Chytraei haeretici imposturas, quas in oratione quadam inseruit, quam de statu ecclesiarum hoc tempore in Graecia, Asia, Africa, Ungaria, Bohemia inscriptam edidit et per Sueciam ac Daniam disseminari curavit* (Ingolstadt, 1583). (This citation appears in Schottenloher, op. cit.)

[27] Alfred Hessel, *A History of Libraries,* trans. Reuben Peiss (Washington, D. C.: Scarecrow Press, 1950), pp. 71, 72.

[28] Quoted in Schmauk, p. 561. On pp. 560, 561, Chytraeus' lengthy (four-paragraph) argument for the authenticity of this document is given in translation.

[29] See above, our text at note 25. Coelestin may have made a mistake, been deceived, or even have himself perpetrated the error.

[30] Schmauk, p. 535.

17

numerous,[31] did not affect its doctrinal teaching. Schmauk is eminently correct when he writes: "That the authors of the Formula of Concord were deceived as to the original German text of the Augsburg Confession, no more proves the lack of authority of the Confession as a confessional standard, or its lack of a fixed doctrinal and general textual form, than the fact that . . . because the New Testament contains certain passages, which are now regarded as spurious on the authority of the best manuscripts, and because texts have been discovered which completely change many of the readings of the old Textus Receptus, it therefore is no longer to be found in standard form, and has only a passing and changeable value for those who believe and confess it." [32]

In 1581 Chytraeus' fame had become so widespread that a request came from Antwerp for his opinion on a catechism; and in 1584 he wrote a rejoinder to Possevinus' polemic, which had been called forth by Chytraeus' influence in the Scandinavian countries.[33]

In his sixty-ninth year Chytraeus succumbed to a concurrence of various diseases; his death at Rostock on June 25, 1600, was, in the common parlance of the time, described as "edifying." Pressel does not exaggerate when he writes: "Durch die ganze protestantische Kirche . . . tönte die Todtenklage: Der letzte Repräsentant des reichsten Jahrhunderts der Weltgeschichte ward im ersten Jahre einer neuen Zeit zu Grabe getragen; der treue Jünger Luthers und Melanchthons zu seinen Vätern versammelt." [34]

[31] G. G. Weber, who established the fact that this copy was not the original, of course made the most of it. According to him, the copy "swarms" (wimmelt) with textual errors (Kritische Gesch. d. Augsb. Konfession [1783 to 1784], 2 vols.; quoted and discussed at length in Schmauk).

[32] Schmauk, p. 562.

[33] For the title of Possevinus' book, see above, note 26. Possevinus, an Italian Jesuit (1534—1611), was a man of wide scholarly interests; during his lifetime he wrote not only on theology but also in the field of bibliography (Bibliotheca selecta), medicine (Causae et remedia pestilentiae), and textual criticism (Apparatus sacer).

[34] Pressel, p. 46. Of the many other works written by Chytraeus, three deserve special mention: (1) Onomasticon theologicum (1557, 1578), "an attempt to combine a theological encyclopedia and a Hebrew dictionary" (Loësche); (2) Oratio de studio theologiae (1562, 1571, 1581, 1707, 1781); (3) De morte et vita aeterna (1581—82), "the first attempt at

Having obtained a general overview of Chytraeus' life, let us consider specifically his labors in behalf of the Formula of Concord. We shall begin with the events immediately following his declaration (in 1558) against the Frankfort Recess.

From January 21 through February 8, 1561, the important Diet at Naumburg (an der Saale) was held; Chytraeus attended as adviser to Duke Ulrich of Mecklenburg.[35] The purpose of the meeting was to achieve Lutheran unity on the basis of the Augsburg Confession, in view of political dangers and the reconvening of the Council of Trent.[36] But which Augsburg Confession was to be used? The original invitation to this Diet of Princes had specified the Invariata edition. But Elector Frederick III of the Palatinate (who later became a Calvinist) preferred the 1540 Variata edition. A compromise was signed by all present except Duke John Frederick of Saxony (son-in-law of Frederick III) and Ulrich of Mecklenburg — both of whom wished the Invariata to be protected against the later errors which had arisen. After John Frederick in anger left the Diet, Duke Ulrich signed the compromise. However, under the guidance of their theologians, all the princes except Frederick III subsequently withdrew their signatures and sided with John Frederick. Chytraeus' part in the Diet was an influential one. It is true that he and Nikolaus Selnecker [37] "spoke mildly of the edition of 1540 and thought to find in it no

a complete eschatology in the Melanchthonian spirit" (Loesche). For a complete list of Chytraeus' writings, classed under the heads "Exegetical Works," "Dogmatic Works," "Philological Works," "Historical Works," etc., see Schütz, III, 471—480. He wrote Biblical commentaries on Genesis through Ruth, Micah, Nahum, Habakkuk, Zechariah, Malachi, Matthew, John, Romans, Timothy and Titus(?), and Revelation.

35 Ulrich III (1527—1603) was the younger brother of Duke Johann Albrecht I (see above, note 13). Heinrich the Peaceable had died in 1552, and Ulrich had demanded further divisions of the ducal lands. (*Allgemeine deutsche Biographie*, XXXIX, 225, 226)

36 For the historical material in this paragraph, I have followed the excellent treatment of the Diet at Naumburg given in Schmauk, pp. 531—533, 552 to 559.

37 Selnecker (Selneccer, Schellenecker), 1530—1592, was one of the great figures in the Lutheran church of the 16th century. His theology was solid; his character was saintly; and his extensive hymn writing included the beautiful "Ach bleib bei uns, Herr Jesu Christ."

variation of the essential doctrine,"[38] but when the issues became clean-cut, and it seemed that basic Lutheran doctrine might be obscured at the Diet, Chytraeus, "as well as the Saxon theologians Mörlin and Stössel, warned against the acceptance of the later editions."[39] Though the Naumburg Diet failed in achieving its specific purpose, it constituted a very significant link in the chain leading to the Formula of Concord.[40]

In 1567 Chytraeus put into writing the results of his university's deliberation on the Weimar Confutation. This Confutation had been formulated in 1558 by the strict (Gnesio-) Lutherans of Ducal Saxony, and — in marked contrast to the Frankfort Recess — it specifically condemned doctrinal views which were not in harmony with orthodox Lutheran teaching.[41] In the Rostock statement the theological faculty, headed by Chytraeus, likewise declared itself categorically against any Calvinist interpretation of the Lord's Supper; and through all the subsequent controversies on this issue the faculty remained of the same viewpoint.

Fifteen seventy-four provided Chytraeus with his opportunity to contribute directly to what would eventually become the Formula of Concord. After Chemnitz had made changes in the "Swabian Concord" forwarded to him from Tübingen by its author, Andreae,[42] Chemnitz in turn sent the document to Chytraeus at Rostock. "The faculty at Rostock was highly respected as the representative of theological learning in Lower Saxony. It had taken the lead in the controversies of the past years. It stood for sound Lutheranism over against wavering Philippism. The leading theologian was Chytraeus, who had studied under Melanchthon, but, like Chemnitz and many

[38] Schmauk, p. 533 (following G. G. Weber — see above, note 31).

[39] Ibid., p. 554 (following C. A. Salig's *Vollständige Historie d. A. C.* [Halle, 1730—35]).

[40] Ibid., p. 559.

[41] Allbeck, pp. 245, 256.

[42] Jacob Andreae (1528—1590) had published in 1573 "Six Christian Sermons, concerning the divisions among the theologians of the Augsburg Confession, as they arose from the year 1548 up to this present 1573d year, how a plain pastor and a common Christian layman who might be scandalized thereby, might be set right through the catechism" (title given in Schmauk, pp. 650, 651, where an extended discussion of the "Sermons" appears). When revised by the author, these "Sermons" became the "Swabian Concord," the foundation document of the Formula of Concord.

other pupils of the Preceptor, did not share his teacher's half-heartedness. Chytraeus acted as the amanuensis of the faculty. He made many changes in the articles laid before him. He preferred to rewrite two articles, the second and seventh." [43] Thus Chytraeus came to be the author of the articles on Free Will and the Lord's Supper in the "Swabian-Saxon Formula" (as it was now called) and to contribute numerous other revisions to it. The fact is, of

[43] J. Fritschel, *The Formula of Concord, Its Origin and Contents* (Philadelphia: Lutheran Publication Society, 1916), p. 102. This author points out, on pp. 102, 112, 146—150, and 194, that Chytraeus was responsible for virtually the whole of Articles II (on Free Will) and VII (on the Lord's Supper). Fritschel also exactly specifies Chytraeus' not insignificant contributions to the other articles of the Formula. (In a note, pp. 103, 104, Fritschel writes: "The Bertelsmann Verlag at Guetersloh was about to publish a comparison of the various stages of the text [of the Formula], presenting a survey of the gradual growth, when the war [i. e., World War I] broke out. This comparison has been composed by the author. The manuscript is still in the author's possession; he hopes to issue it sometime in the near future." This valuable MS. was unfortunately never published. In his obituary for Professor Fritschel which appeared in the *Kirchliche Zeitschrift*, LXV:12 [December 1941], 706, 707, M. Reu stated that in 1932 he received Fritschel's "voluminous" {umfangreichen} manuscripts dealing with the Formula; but all trace of these seems to have disappeared. Dr. Bernard J. Holm, professor of historical theology, Wartburg Seminary, has for several years made every effort to trace these manuscripts among relatives of Dr. Fritschel and of Dr. Reu but has so far been unsuccessful. Wartburg Seminary has Fritschel's personal copy of Heinrich Heppe's *Der Text der bergischen Concordienformel* [Marburg: J. A. Koch, 1857], with his numerous annotations [some in color] indicating sources; this volume entered the Wartburg Library among the books received in the Reu bequest.) That Articles II and VII of the Formula were the most significant historically is clear from the historical situation which gave rise to the Formula. "The debate which ensued over Melanchthon's synergism issued in Article II of the Formula of Concord, in which Melanchthon's stand is repudiated. . . . Thus the traditional interpretation is correct when it sees the Formula as the defeat of Melanchthon in the Lutheran Church" (Jaroslav Pelikan, *From Luther to Kierkegaard* [St. Louis: Concordia, 1950], p. 44). On Article VII (the Lord's Supper), Charles Porterfield Krauth writes: "This was by preeminence the question which led to the preparation of the Formula, and it is answered with peculiar distinctness and fulness" *(The Conservative Reformation and Its Theology* [Philadelphia: Lippincott, 1871], pp. 314, 315). Two older works still worth consulting for the history and theology of the Formula are: Heinrich Heppe, *Geschichte der lutherischen Concordienformel* (Marburg: Elwert, 1857), which serves as Vol. III of Heppe's *Geschichte des deutschen Protestantismus in den Jahren 1555—1581;* and F. H. R. Frank, *Theologie der Konkordienformel* (Erlangen: Bläsing, 1858 ff.).

course, that Articles II and VII were not allowed to stand exactly as Chytraeus had written them; Chytraeus had a tendency to be "very voluminous," [44] and the "Swabian-Saxon Formula" had become much longer than Andreae's original draft. The result was some excision and condensation, and Article II suffered most; but even in the latter case "nothing essential was expunged; only nonessential parts were omitted." [45]

The next vital step in the creation of the Formula of Concord occurred in the Castle of Hartenfels at Torgau from May 28 to June 7, 1576. The seventeen Lutheran theologians (including Chytraeus) selected by the various states to meet there [46] were instructed by Elector Augustus of Saxony to propose a doctrinal statement which could be submitted to all Lutheran princes for approval. The bases of their activity were to be the "Swabian-Saxon Formula," and the "Maulbronn Formula" (a document prepared for the Elector Augustus early in 1576 by which he might judge the orthodoxy of his theologians). "Andreae had suggested to the elector that the Maulbrunn Formula should be made the basis of the new confession, since it was so very simple and yet to the point; but Chemnitz and Chytraeus preferred to use the Swabian-Saxon Concordia as the basis. This latter document was known by this time to all outside of the Saxonies, and had been approved universally, while the Maulbrunn Formula was known to few outside of the authors. They suggested that suitable parts from the Maulbrunn Formula might be inserted into the Swabian-Saxon agreement. This motion prevailed." [47] The completed "Torgau Book" was transmitted to the Elector on June 7, and a thanksgiving service was held in which Selnecker [48] preached.

[44] Fritschel, p. 102.

[45] Ibid., p. 146. Chytraeus complained in his letters that "everything" he wrote was cast out, but Fritschel makes clear that he was exaggerating (cf. note 18 above). In Fritschel, pp. 146—150, one finds in English translation (1) Andreae's draft of Article II (Chytraeus used "only a few fragments" of this draft of the Article), (2) a selection from that portion of Chytraeus' Article II which was later condensed at Torgau and Bergen.

[46] The seventeen are named in Fritschel, p. 108.

[47] Fritschel, p. 109. The additions (from the "Maulbronn Formula") made at Torgau to the "Swabian-Saxon Formula" are given by Fritschel, pp. 109, 110.

[48] See above, note 37.

Chytraeus was also present at the most important (May 1577) Bergen Cloister meeting [49] which produced the "Bergen Book," or final draft of the Formula of Concord. At the May meeting the *censurae* (opinions) which had been received from many quarters with regard to the "Torgau Book" were evaluated and brought to a final vote by the theologians taking part (Andreae, Chemnitz, Selnecker, Chytraeus, and Musculus).[50] "Chytraeus felt offended that so many changes were made in the articles of which he was the author. . . . This had been done to shorten the document." [51]

In spite of any feelings of dissatisfaction which he may have carried away with him from Bergen, Chytraeus proceeded to work with all his might for the universal adoption of the Formula. He defended its teachings on original sin against the Flacians, and he took part in the conventions at Tangermünde (1578) and at Jüterbock (1579).[52] When on June 25, 1580, the *Book of Concord* was finally published and the Elector Augustus celebrated it by minting a coin showing himself in full armor on the storm-tossed ship of the church,[53] Chytraeus might legitimately have held such a coin in his hand and visualized himself as one of the helmsmen of that ship.

Chytraeus' "De Sacrificiis"

The relation between Chytraeus' obscurity in our time and the dearth of modern translations of his writings has been emphasized at the outset of this Introduction. The present work offers

[49] Fritschel, p. 111, points out that "two (perhaps three) meetings were held at Bergen, near Magdeburg" in 1577. Schmauk, p. 659, writes: "At the last convention toward the end of May, they quickly agreed on the chief part, eventually the second part of the work, *The Solid Declaration*."

[50] Andreas Musculus (Meusel), 1514—1581. For a brief biographical sketch, see Krauth, p. 311. Schmauk (p. 658) also includes Christoph Körner (1518—1594), "the Eye of the University" (of Frankfort a. O.).

[51] Fritschel, p. 112. (But see above, my text at note 45.) For the changes made in the "Torgau Book" at Bergen, see Fritschel, pp. 112, 113.

[52] "When . . . a number of conferences with those withholding their names had failed to convince them, the theologians who had completed the Formula assembled at Jüterbock in January, 1579, and composed the Preface, which was afterward revised at Bergen in February, and again at Jüterbock in June, and then received the subscription of the rulers and states" (H. E. Jacobs, ed., *Book of Concord* [Philadelphia: G. W. Frederick, 1882—83], II, 61).

[53] Schaff, I, 311.

the first translation from the Latin into any other language of his treatise On Sacrifice. Why was the *De sacrificiis* chosen for such treatment rather than one of the many other publications of this prolific author?

Three criteria governed the choice. First, the work translated should be the product of Chytraeus' university lectures and relate as closely as possible to his actual classroom teaching. Too few illustrations of Reformation university instruction are available to the English-reading world. Second, the work should exemplify Chytraeus' central interest — Biblical theology. Third, the work should pertain in some definite way to the author's contribution to the Formula of Concord.

On all three counts the *De sacrificiis* is a happy choice. It was published as a prolegomenon to Chytraeus' Commentary on Leviticus (1st ed., Wittenberg, 1569; another ed., ibid., 1575; republished in his collected exegetical works, ibid., 1590; and reissued in his *Opera omnia,* Leipzig, 1599).[54] His biographer writes: "This Commentary on Leviticus exceeds in size the expositions which our author previously published on Genesis and Exodus; this is due to the inclusion not only of the Latin [Biblical] text but especially of a splendid *(luculentam)* 108-page prefatory treatise on the sacrifices of the Old and New Testaments."[55] Although the title page of the *In Leviticum* does not contain the expression "ex praelectionibus Davidis Chytraei," which appears as part of the titles of many of his exegetical works, it is evident that the work originated in the classroom. The best evidence of this is the author's frequent use of the term "auditores" (which, however, for the sake of our present public, we have rendered "readers" in the

---

[54] The first edition (from which the present translation has been made) is not listed in the British Museum *Catalogue,* the *Catalogue général* of the Bibliothèque Nationale, or the National Union Catalog at the Library of Congress. My personal copy of it was obtained through the antiquarian book trade in New York City. Harvard has a copy of the 1575 edition (which, however, has been missing for many years), and Concordia Seminary (St. Louis) owns that volume of the 1599 collected works which contains the *De Sacrificiis.*

[55] Schütz, I, 315. Schütz goes on to criticize rather severely (and unfairly) the Leviticus commentary proper for not containing insights provided by the OT scholarship of a later day (the 17th and early 18th centuries). It is noteworthy that Schütz viewed the *De sacrificiis* as such a separable unit that he gave it its own entry in the subject index at the end of Vol. IV.

translation); other evidences are the didactic admonitions to "the studious" and "the young," and emphatic repetitions which are so characteristic of a lecturer's style. By translating the first edition of On Sacrifice and appending prominent variata from the last edition (rather than the reverse procedure), we hope that it will be possible most effectively to convey the fresh atmosphere in which the material was first presented.

A survey of the contents of the *De sacrificiis* will leave no doubt that it should be classed as a work of Biblical theology; through its pages our author is able to demonstrate his grasp of both Old Testament and New Testament scholarship and to relate these to the doctrinal issues of current relevance in his own time. The first publication of the work took place eight years after Chytraeus had become a regular professor of theology at Rostock and two years after he had led his university in supporting the Weimar Confutation.[56] He was not to contribute to the "Swabian-Saxon Formula" until 1574. Thus we have in the *De sacrificiis* an example of his mature exegetical skill; but in this case his work is not motivated primarily by the controversial situations which would later assume such importance for him.

The connection between the *De sacrificiis* and the Formula of Concord lies in the fact, previously stated, that the Formula article for which Chytraeus was most fully and finally responsible is Article VII on the Lord's Supper.[57] Numerous parallels, both in style and content, are evident. No reader of the *De sacrificiis*, for example, could help recognizing as familiar such statements in Article VII as these:

In the institution of His last will and testament and of His abiding covenant and union, He [Christ] uses no flowery language but the most appropriate, simple, indubitable, and clear words, just as He does in all the articles of faith and in the institution of other covenant-signs and

[56] The first edition's "Epistola Dedicatoria" (written by Nathan Chytraeus, David's younger brother and a fine scholar in his own right) is dated at Rostock, December 11 ("3. Idus"), 1568. Chytraeus apparently completed the book in 1568 and, before departing for Austria at the beginning of December, left it with his brother to be seen through the press.

[57] Those paragraph-sections of Article VII which are entirely or almost entirely Chytraeus' work are: 1—3, 6—19, 33—90, 99—103, 107—128 (Fritschel, p. 194).

signs of grace or sacraments, such as circumcision, the many kinds of sacrifice in the Old Testament, and holy Baptism. And so that no misunderstanding could creep in, he explained things more clearly by adding the words, "given for you, shed for you." [58]

This spiritual eating . . . is precisely faith — namely, that we hear, accept with faith, and appropriate to ourselves the Word of God, in which Christ, true God and man, together with all the benefits that He has acquired for us by giving His body for us into death and by shedding His blood for us (that is to say, the grace of God, forgiveness of sins, righteousness, and everlasting life), is presented — and that we rest indomitably, with certain trust and confidence, on this comforting assurance that we have a gracious God and eternal salvation for the sake of Jesus Christ, and hold to it in all difficulty and temptation.[59]

On Sacrifice should bring about much greater appreciation of the fact (too often overlooked in the present day) that no better foundation for systematic theology and confessional churchmanship can be laid than that provided by thorough Biblical studies.

*　　*　　*

A word perhaps needs to be said in anticipation of certain objections that will inevitably be brought to bear against the republication in translation of Chytraeus' treatise. Three such objections ought to be mentioned here. The first is that a work in Biblical theology scarcely deserves to be reread when it harks back to the predocumentary criticism era and obviously presupposes a plenary view of Biblical inspiration. The second objection is that a work which in many ways reflects an Anselmic conception of the atonement ought not to be raised again to a position of theological prominence. The third argument is that the scholastic methodology of post-Luther, 16th- and 17th-century Lutheran "Orthodoxy" would better be buried than re-emphasized.

[58] Par. 50. Trans. Arthur C. Piepkorn in *The Book of Concord,* ed. Theodore G. Tappert (Philadelphia: Muhlenberg, 1959), p. 578.

[59] Par. 62 (ibid., p. 581). A particularly telling stylistic comparison is provided by the involute sentence in paragraphs 43—48 (best seen in Jacobs' translation, op. cit., I, 608—610, where the original German is not broken up into so many short sentences in the English translation).

Let us briefly consider these objections, beginning with the last. In note 70 to Chytraeus' text an attempt is made to point out that our author is, in his methodological approach, far closer to Luther and the Reformers than to the developed "Orthodoxy" manifested in the great dogmatic productions of the 17th century. However, it is readily admitted that Chytraeus frequently employed basic scholastic categories. The question is: What is wrong with that? Scholastic principles of analysis were widely accepted in his time as a valuable technique for getting at the heart of rational questions. To use the best philosophical insights of one's time is the strength, not the downfall, of a theologian, unless, of course, he perverts special revelation by so doing. I must quote in agreement Paul Tillich's flat assertion: "No theologian should be taken seriously as a theologian, even if he is a great Christian and a great scholar, if his work shows that he does not take philosophy seriously." [60] Moreover, logic (whether scholastic or otherwise) has a peculiarly necessitarian character about it. Even those (such as the Barthians and Kierkegaardians) who argue against the relevance of logic and logical distinction in theology, must use logic to do so. As Emerson said of Brahma, "When me they fly, I am the wings."

With regard to the presence of Anselmism in the *De sacrificiis,* two points should be made. (1) This is by no means the only (though it is admittedly the strongest) atonement motif presented in the work. For example, Chytraeus devotes a lengthy paragraph (beginning at our note 156) to the reasons why the Redeemer had to be God in the full sense, not merely representative man, and argues that otherwise He would not have had the power to "bruise the head of the serpent (that is, destroy the works of the devil)." Here our author relies on patristic authors (Athanasius and Irenaeus are specifically cited), and more than a trace of the *Christus Victor* concept is certainly in evidence.[61] But (2) the Aulén approach, so widely accepted today, deserves close scrutiny. An examination

[60] Paul Tillich, *Biblical Religion and the Search for Ultimate Reality* (Chicago: University of Chicago Press, 1955), pp. 7, 8.

[61] "The teaching of Irenaeus is clear and consistent and forms a thoroughly typical example of that view of the Atonement which we have called the Classic Idea" (Gustaf Aulén, *Christus Victor,* trans. A. G. Hebert [New York: Macmillan, 1956], p. 34). "Athanasius is in no way forsaking the classic point of view" (ibid., p. 56).

of the Appendix to the present publication may well convince the reader that Chytraeus' study of sacrifice on the basis of *sola Scriptura* (with a natural emphasis on Hebrews and the Old Testament) could not but differ radically from an approach based on history of dogma and *Motivforschung.*

Coming now to Chytraeus' view of inspiration, we readily concede that though he was no Biblical literalist (see note 92 to his text), he did believe in the plenary inspiration of the Scriptures, quoted freely and in juxtaposition from Old Testament and New, and had no notion of the documentary ("higher") criticism which would arise with Witter and Astruc well over a century after his death.[62] Does this vitiate his treatment of Biblical sacrifice? Many will differ with me, I have no doubt, when I answer this question in the negative. There are two aspects to Biblical study: the determination of documentary origins and the meaning which ur-fragments had in their original setting, and the significance that the resultant Scriptural writings came to have for Christ, the apostles, and the church. When the former aspect is confused with the latter, Biblical study inevitably suffers.[63] If the canonical Scriptures comprise a special revelation from God Himself, then they can (and must) be studied as a resultant unity and totality. As William James so effectively pointed out early in his *Varieties of Religious Experience,* the historical origin of something does not necessarily determine its ultimate value. These considerations make it possible for us to apply to our author W. H. Cooper's recent remarks on the use of the Old Testament by Chemnitz, Chytraeus' co-worker on the Formula of Concord:

> Because of his own time and place he is totally unconcerned about items of literary and historical criticism which fascinate and often sidetrack the modern investigator. He is innocent of archaeology. He is oblivious to

[62] Cf. Robert Preus, *The Inspiration of Scripture: A Study of the Theology of the Seventeenth-Century Lutheran Dogmaticians,* 2d ed. (Edinburgh: Oliver and Boyd, 1957).

[63] "The critical work of the Wellhausen school moves methodologically in a haze, because it is insufficiently aware of the difference between empirical, philological work and the interpretations put on its results." (Eric Voegelin, *Israel and Revelation,* in *Order and History,* I [Baton Rouge: Louisiana State University Press, 1956], 153.)

the comparative study of religions. Without the apparatus of modern Old Testament scholarship except for his knowledge of Hebrew, he is also free of its encumbrances and liabilities. As a consequence he speedily gets to the heart of Old Testament teaching as it concerns the vital subjects about which he must write; and in this practical use of the Old Testament he shows a mastery and a familiarity with it in detail which might well be the envy of the contemporary theologian.[64]

Several concluding remarks on the technical side are now in order. As mentioned earlier, the present translation follows the 1569 (first) edition of the *De sacrificiis*,[65] rather than the last (1599) edition.[66] Since it is usual to present as the basic text that which represents the author's final intention, a word of *apologia* is perhaps needed here. My approach follows the principles set down by Professor Morize: "In a great number of cases it is well to choose the first form of an important work"; and: "The editor's endeavor should be to select and reproduce the text that has the greatest historical significance." [67] The 1569 edition is of "greatest historical significance" because it is closest in time to the events of the Reformation and to the delivery of the material in lecture form and because it reflects the thinking of the author prior to his work in behalf of the Formula of Concord. Moreover, it is fuller than the 1599 edition, since in the latter the final section,

[64] W. H. Cooper, "Martin Chemnitz on Justification; with Special Reference to His Use of the Old Testament," pt. 2, *Northwestern Seminary Bulletin,* XXXV:5 (January 1960), 8.

[65] *In Leviticum, seu Tertium Librum Mosis, complectentem unius mensis historiam, videlicet: Leges de sacrificiis et discrimine mundorum et immundorum, et res alias in Ecclesia populi Israel gestas, primo mense anni secundi post exitum ex Aegypto . . . autore D. Davide Chytraeo* (Witebergae, 1569). [16], 582 pp. The *De sacrificiis* covers (numbered) pp. 1—108.

[66] *Davidis Chytraei Operum tomus primus. Continens enarrationes in quinque libros Mosis . . . coniunctim ac emendatè editos . . .* (Lipsiae, impensis Henningi Grosii Bibliop., 1599). In-folio. [10], 220, 542, [9] pp. The Commentary on Deuteronomy is bound ahead of those on Genesis-Numbers. The *De sacrificiis* appears on pp. 329—356 of the second numbered section.

[67] André Morize, *Problems and Methods of Literary History* (Boston: Ginn and Company, 1922), pp. 53, 54.

taken over from the Commentary on Matthew, is dropped (see note 284 to the text, and Variata reading ⁰⁰). Aside from this difference, however, the variations between the two editions are quite minor,[68] and those of substantive character in the last edition have been indicated by superscript letters in the text and recorded in a brief apparatus at the end of this book.

It is hoped that the rather full grammatical and philological notes to the text will not disturb the reader interested only in the historical and theological aspects of Chytraeus' work. The lack of such notes in most translations of Reformation authors appears to me to constitute a distinct scholarly lacuna; I shall be happy if the inclusion of notes of this kind here removes from others some of the prevailing hesitancy to take up the editing and translating of 16th- and 17th-century Protestant theological authors. It should not be difficult for the nonspecialist to pass over those notes of little interest to him; and I will be surprised if even the layman does not find much to whet his appetite among the many editorial annotations.

I wish, finally, to express appreciation to Robert Preus of Concordia Seminary, St. Louis, whose stimulating lecture, "Quenstedt on Justification" (delivered at the second annual Symposium on Seventeenth-Century Lutheranism, June 12, 1959) was of help in the present study; to W. D. Allbeck of Hamma Divinity School, and Arthur C. Piepkorn of Concordia Seminary, who provided valuable suggestions on a number of difficult points; to T. A. Kantonen of Hamma Divinity School, who read in preliminary form the Appendix of this work; to Walter J. Kukkonen of Chicago Lutheran Theological Seminary, who gave the editorial Introduction a preliminary reading; to E. E. Flack, dean emeritus, Hamma Divinity School, whose constant encouragement has been of inestimable value; to Robert Rosenthal, head of the University of Chicago Library's Department of Special Collections, and to Edgar Krentz, librarian of Concordia Seminary, for their many kindnesses;

---

[68] For example, some obvious typographical errors in the first edition are corrected in the last, while some other errors are introduced in the final edition. Small paragraphs tend to be combined into larger paragraphs in the 1599 ed., and "etc.," "scilicet," "hoc est," and the like are frequently dropped.

to Mrs. June Lawson, formerly secretary to the dean, University of Chicago Divinity School, for her competent and faithful typing of the manuscript; and, lastly, to the third annual Symposium on Seventeenth-Century Lutheranism, for honoring me with an invitation to read this Introduction to the *De Sacrificiis* as a paper in 1960.

John Warwick Montgomery

I must repeat what I said in beginning, that the translator of Homer ought steadily to keep in mind where lies the real test of the success of his translation, what judges he is to try to satisfy. He is to try to satisfy *scholars,* because scholars alone have the means of really judging him. A scholar may be a pedant, it is true, and then his judgment will be worthless; but a scholar may also have poetical feeling, and then he can judge him truly; whereas all the poetical feeling in the world will not enable a man who is not a scholar to judge him truly.

Matthew Arnold, *On Translating Homer*

No one can understand the word "cheese" unless he has a non-linguistic acquaintance with cheese.

Bertrand Russell, "Logical Positivism"

I have done it [the German Bible] as a service to the dear Christians and to the honor of One who sits above, who blesses me so much every hour of my life that, if I had translated a thousand times as much or as diligently, I still should not deserve to live a single hour or have a sound eye. All that I am and have is of His grace and mercy, nay, of His dear blood and His bitter sweat. Therefore, God willing, all of it shall serve to His honor, joyfully and sincerely. . . . And I am repaid all too richly if only one single Christian recognizes me as a faithful workman. . . . Still, I would be a doctor, nay, a wonderful doctor; and that name they shall not take from me till the Last Day, that I know for sure.

Martin Luther, *On Translating: An Open Letter*

I

PRELIMINARY CONSIDERATIONS

A. *Overview of the Christian Doctrine of Sacrifice*

The foundation of our salvation and of all religion, and the basis of the Christian faith, is the doctrine of the priesthood and [a] sacrifice of God's Son, our Lord and Redeemer Jesus Christ, who was offered to God in our behalf on the altar of the cross. This act alone earned for us the remission of sins, righteousness, and everlasting life; and on it alone can the faith and prayers of the pious and one's hope of eternal life safely and peacefully rely in the consciousness of God's wrath, in the anguish of repentance, in all perils, and in the agony of death.

Now the prime sources from which the doctrine of Christ's sacrifice should be derived are God's two supreme characteristics: His *justice* and His *mercy.* For since God is truly and unchangeably just, He maintains this immutable and eternal standard: rational creatures must either be righteous and perfectly conform to divine righteousness and goodness, or undergo an adequate punishment and suffer horrible destruction if they sin and do not live in accord with the standard of divine Law. Therefore, when the first human beings transgressed (on whom God had bestowed the treasure of complete righteousness for their own benefit and that of all their posterity), God's absolutely just judgment demanded that both the transgressors and the entire human race born of them perish in eternal retribution. But in His boundless mercy the Son of God interceded, pleading with the eternal Father for human kind; and in order to satisfy God's eternal justice He even offered Himself for punishment and recompense. So by a remarkable balance of divine justice and mercy this admirable plan was put into effect: God's Son would take on human nature and become a sacrificial victim, thus placating the utterly just wrath of God and restoring righteousness and eternal salvation to the human race. Because of this sacrifice of God's Son, all the elect in the entire history of the

33

world have obtained the remission of their sins and have inherited everlasting life; as Acts 4:12 says: "There is none other name under heaven whereby we must be saved." [1]

And in order that men might be admonished and instructed concerning the sacrifice of Christ, God instituted animal sacrifices immediately after His first creatures had been drawn back to Him. The latter sacrifices by no means possessed a worth meriting the remission of sins; they were types — copies — representations of the true sacrifice of God's Son. Through His sacrifice alone God procured for us, on the one hand, eternal redemption from divine wrath, from sin, from the curse of the Law, from the tyranny of the devil, and from eternal death; and on the other, reconciliation with Himself, righteousness, and everlasting life and glory.

I shall now proceed briefly and methodically to expound the sum total of the teaching on sacrifice given in the Old and New Testaments.[2]

B. *The Vocabulary of Sacrifice*

Since I am about to set forth the essentials of the doctrine of priesthood and [b] sacrifice, I shall first explain the terms used to refer to these concepts.

[1] Throughout the translation, Scripture quotations are given according to the Authorized Version (since it represents the great literary version of the Bible in English); when a text quotation varies from the latter, the AV is altered accordingly, and in the case of a conflict a note points out the divergence and relates it to the Gk. original. The Biblical verse numbers included in the translation have been inserted editorially; although Biblical verse divisions had been introduced in 1551 (in the Gk. NT printed at Geneva by Robert Estienne/Stephanus), they were not commonly employed until sometime later, and our text (1569) relies on chapter numbers exclusively. It will be noted, however, that we have not inserted partial verse divisions (a, b, etc.). Where chapter or verse numeration differs in the Heb., Septuagint, and AV, we have in all cases followed the AV; such variation occurs particularly in the Psalms.

[2] This sentence is translated in abbreviated form (a clause is dropped), and the sentence following it in the text has been entirely omitted in the translation. In the omitted sentence and clause, Chytraeus relates the treatise On Sacrifice to his Leviticus commentary, which it introduced; as such, the clause and sentence are not germane to the present translation.

(1) The most common word for sacrifice employed by the Hebrews is קָרְבָּן (qorbān),[3] that is, "offering," or "gift offered to God," from קָרַב {qārabh}, "he has drawn near," whose Hiphil[4] (הִקְרִיב {hiqrîbh}), consequently means "he has carried forward," "he has offered." This word qorbān in fact appears in the New Testament as well as the Old. Mark 7:11: ἐὰν εἴπῃ ἄνθρωπος τῷ πατρὶ ἢ τῇ μητρί· κορβᾶν, ὅ ἐστιν δῶρον, ὃ ἐὰν ἐξ ἐμοῦ ὠφεληθῇς [καλῶς ποιεῖ] ("If a man shall say to his father or mother, It is Corban, that is to say, a gift offered to God or something dedicated to the temple, by whatsoever thou mightest be profited by me, he does well").[5] Here Christ rebuked the hypocrisy and avarice of the Pharisees, who taught that holier works and more God-pleasing worship were performed by those who gave their money and property to the temple and the priests than by those who used their substance in dutifully caring for their parents. Matt. 27:6: "It is not lawful for to put them into the corbona," that is, into

---

[3] The "gen[eral] term for all kinds of offering" (BDB 898). Throughout his *De sacrificiis,* our author uses unpointed Heb.; the addition of Masoretic pointing in the translation is thus editorial. Chytraeus generally (but not always) provides a transliteration of the Heb. words he uses; we have, in all cases where individual words (but not clauses or sentences) appear in Heb. script in the text, given transliterations according to the most common modern phonetic system. Modern Heb. consonantal type has been employed in the translation; no attempt has been made pedantically to reproduce the peculiarities of the Heb. text type (e. g., the use of ח for both ח and ה). Moreover, silent correction of a few obvious typographical *lapsus* in Heb. words has been made in the translation.

[4] The causative active of the Heb. verb.

[5] Here, as in some other instances, our author gives an expanded translation for the sake of greater clarity. Gk. typography, orthography, breathings, and punctuation have been consistently modernized by the present editor, but Chytraeus' readings of the Biblical text have not been altered. All textual comparisons are based on Nestle's *Novum Testamentum Graece et Latine,* 18th ed. (Stuttgart: Privileg. Württ. Bibelanstalt, 1957). Archaic ligatures, whether Gk. or Lat., have been expanded by use of the tables in G. F. von Ostermann's *Manual of Foreign Languages for the Use of Librarians, Bibliographers, Research Workers, Editors, Translators, and Printers,* 4th ed. (New York: Central Book Co., 1952), pp. 105—108, 165; and *Wolfgang Fuggers Schreibbüchlein . . . Vollständige Faksimile-Ausgabe des 1553 in Nürnberg erschienenen Werkes,* ed. Fritz Funke (Leipzig: Harrassowitz, 1958), has also proved a useful tool.

the coffer in which they kept gifts offered to God. Latin translators of Leviticus have rendered the term *qorbān* sometimes as "offering" {*oblatio*}, sometimes as "victim" {*victima*}, and sometimes as "sacrificial animal" {*hostia*}, without discrimination.

(2) זֶבַח (*zebhaḥ*) is a sacrifice of a slaughtered beast or victim.[6c] Lev. 3:1: אִם־זֶבַח שְׁלָמִים קָרְבָּנוֹ ("If his oblation be a sacrificial animal or sacrifice of restoration or peace offering . . ."). The word is derived from the root זָבַח (*zābhaḥ*), which means "to slaughter," and, by synecdoche, "to offer slaughtered animals to God," and in general "to sacrifice." Whence מִזְבֵּחַ (*mizbēaḥ*), "an altar."

(3) מִנְחָה (*minḥāh*)[7] refers to an offering or sacrifice of food or grain.[8] This type of sacrifice is described in Lev. 2. The word is derived either from the root נחה [√NḤH],[7] "he has brought forward, offered," or from מנח [√MNḤ], "gift."[9] The latter is the source of "manna," the name given to the food of the Israelites.[10]

6 "The common and most ancient sacrifice, whose essential rite was eating the flesh of the victim at a feast in which the god of the clan shared by receiving the blood and fat pieces" (BDB 257).

7 The text has ת's (th's) for ח's (ḥ's) in these words; correction has been made in the translation.

8 The so-called "meat offering" of the AV. See below, section II. A. 4.

9 "The etymology of this word that has been commonly accepted would give it as its original meaning *gift;* it is said to be from the root מנח. . . . An alternative etymology was proposed centuries ago by Abu-l-walid, was criticized by Ḳimḥi, dropped out of view, and has of late been revived, partly on the ground of fresh evidence. According to this theory, מנחה is from the root נחה, meaning *to lead, guide,* and would therefore have meant originally *something led,* and when the word received a ritual force, something led to the altar. . . . When due weight is given to all these considerations it seems to me hazardous to deny that מנחה in the earliest Hebrew literature meant (sacrificial) *gift;* whatever its etymology and its exact original meaning, by the eighth or ninth century to the Hebrew mind it called up the idea of gift as well when it was used of what was brought to God as when it was used of what was brought to kings." (G. B. Gray, *Sacrifice in the Old Testament* [Oxford: Clarendon Press, 1925], pp. 14—17. This book, which is considered the standard English work on the OT sacrificial system, can be consulted with profit for collateral information on the various matters, philological and theological, discussed by Chytraeus in sections I. B. 1. and II. A.)

10 Semitic language scholarship today recognizes no etymological connection here.

(4) אִשֶּׁה ('ishsheh) is a sacrifice which fire consumes, from אֵשׁ {'ēsh}, "fire." Whence the Greek word ἑστία, and the Latin Vesta.[11]

(5) קְטֹרֶת (qᵉṭōreth)[12] signifies "incense," "perfume," from קִטֵּר (qiṭṭēr), "he has burned in sacrifice,"[13] or "he has burned incense."

2. GREEK

(1) The most common Greek designation for sacrifice is θυσία, from the verb θύειν or θύεσθαι (from which θῦμα, θύος, and θυμίαμα are also derived).[14] It originally referred to producing a fragrance or giving forth a pleasing, very sweet-smelling odor. Thus the raging spirit's ardor or passion is called θυμός.[15] When, consequently, we read that all sacrifices ought to produce an odor acceptable to God and disseminate it over a wide area (that is, please God and make Him known and worshiped by many), the verb θύειν has been generalized to mean "sacrifice," or "offer to God." For example, Thucydides says that all the people of Attica, in their very great festival to Zeus Meilichius (the festival they call the Diasia), πανδημεὶ θύειν οὐχ ἱερεῖα ἀλλὰ θύματα ἐπιχώρια (do not sacrifice priestly[d] victims or animals but offer delicacies peculiar to that region).[16] The learned will recall Isocrates' saying:

[11] ἑστία = Vesta = "hearth/altar/goddess-guardian of the hearth."

[12] In the translation, ת (th) has been corrected to ט (t) in this word. Also, the ḥōlem has been changed from plena to defectiva in accord with Masoretic usage here; Chytraeus may have been thinking of קְטוֹרָה in Deut. 33:10.

[13] The text has adolevit for adoluit.

[14] The latter three nouns are synonyms, meaning "sacrifice," and, as Chytraeus says, derive from θύειν (middle passive θύεσθαι).

[15] θυμός ("soul/spirit/wrath") is derived not from θύειν = "to sacrifice," but from the homonymous θύειν = "to rush/storm/rage."

[16] Chytraeus quotes Thucydides' History of the Peloponnesian War, I. cxxvi. 6. The full sentence from which the quotation has been taken reads: "The Athenians also have a festival in honor of Zeus Meilichius, the Diasia, as it is called, a very great festival celebrated outside the city, whereat all the people offer sacrifices, many making offerings peculiar to the country instead of victims" (Thucydides, with an English tr. by Charles Forster Smith, I [London: Heinemann; Cambridge, Mass.: Harvard University Press (Loeb Classical Library), 1928], 210, 211). A scholiast suggests that the "offerings peculiar to the country" consisted of cakes (πέμματα) made in the forms of animals (ibid.).

θῦμα κάλλιστον καὶ θεραπείαν θεοῦ μεγίστην εἶναι, ἐὰν ὡς βέλτιστον καὶ δικαιότατον σεαυτὸν παρέχῃς ("The best sacrifice and the greatest act of worship to God takes place when you present your very self to God in the best and most righteous condition").[17]

(2) προσφορά is an "offering"; the word comes from προσφέρω.[18]

(3) ἱερός is a general term meaning "sacred," or "consecrated to God." ἱερουργεῖν means not only "to offer victims" but in general "to celebrate sacred occasions," "participate in sacred activities," "teach the Gospel," and "conduct sacred worship" — as Paul writes that he ἱερουργεῖ τὸ εὐαγγέλιον τοῦ θεοῦ [is ministering the Gospel of God], Rom. 15:16.

3. LATIN

(1) It follows that among ecclesiastical Latin writers "sacrifice" {sacrificium} is synonymous with "performing sacred acts,"[e] "attending sacred functions," "teaching and learning the Gospel," "praying to God," "giving thanks," "offering the sacrificial animals commanded by God," "observing sacred rites," and "obeying God in accordance with all His commands." As Augustine says: Every good and God-pleasing work which is done for His sake and directed to Him is called a sacrifice. So also the administration of

[17] Isocrates, the Athenian orator (436—338 B.C.), makes this statement in his oration *To Nicocles*, 20. The complete sentence is as follows: "In the worship of the gods, follow the example of your ancestors, but believe that the noblest sacrifice and the greatest devotion is to show yourself in the highest degree a good and just man; for such men have greater hope of enjoying a blessing from the gods than those who slaughter many victims" (*Isocrates*, with an English tr. by George Norlin, I [London: Heinemann; New York: Putnam (Loeb Classical Library), 1928], 50 to 53). It will be noted that Chytraeus makes the passage refer to "God" (singular) rather than, as in the original, to "gods" (plural). The "hope" of which Isocrates speaks is that of "life beyond this life" (ibid., p. 28, note b). Chytraeus would probably have agreed with C. S. Lewis that such noble sentiments in pagan authors manifest a Natural Law of objective value (*The Abolition of Man* [New York: Macmillan, 1947], especially the "Appendix"; cf. Rom. 1:18-20, 32; 2:14, 15; Apology of the Augsburg Confession, II. iv. 7; Formula of Concord, I. vi. 2; II. vi. 5).

[18] "I bring to/offer."

the Lord's Supper is by the majority of the fathers [19] referred to as a sacrifice.[1]

(2) "The *victim* is so called because it is felled by a *victorious* right hand; the *hostia* [sacrificial victim] takes its name from conquered *hostes* [foes]." [20]

[19] Here Chytraeus alludes to Augustine's *City of God*, x. 6: "There is, then, a true sacrifice in every work which unites us in a holy communion with God, that is, in every work that is aimed at the final Good in which alone we can be truly blessed. That is why even mercy shown to our fellow men is not a sacrifice unless it is done for God. A sacrifice, even though it is done or offered by man, is something divine — which is what the ancient Latins meant by the word *sacrificium*. . . . Our body, too, is a sacrifice when, for God's sake, we chasten it, as we ought, by temperance. . . . The Apostle exhorts us to this when he says: 'I exhort you, therefore, brethren, by the mercy of God to present your bodies as a sacrifice, living, holy, pleasing to God — your spiritual service' [Rom. 12:1]. If, then, the body, which is less than the soul and which the soul uses as a servant or a tool, is a sacrifice when it is used well and rightly for the service of God, how much more so is the soul when it offers itself to God. . . . This is what the Apostle implies in the following verse: 'And be not conformed to this world, but be transformed in the newness of your mind, that you may discern what is the good and acceptable and perfect will of God' [Rom. 12:2]. . . . Therefore, true sacrifices are works of mercy done to ourselves or our neighbor and directed to God" (Saint Augustine, *The City of God, Books VIII to XVI*, trans. Walsh and Monahan [New York: Fathers of the Church, 1952], pp. 125, 126). The Latin text of this passage may be found in J.-P. Migne, ed., *Patrologiae cursus completus . . . series Latina*, XLI (Paris, 1900), cols. 283, 284. Augustine concludes the *City of God*, x. 6, with the following words: "Such is the sacrifice of Christians: 'We, the many, are one body in Christ' [Rom. 12:5]. This is the Sacrifice, as the faithful understand, which the Church continues to celebrate in the sacrament of the altar, in which it is clear to the Church that she herself is offered in the very offering she makes to God" (op. cit., p. 127; Migne, loc. cit.). The application of the term "sacrifice" to the Lord's Supper is discussed by our author in some detail at the close of his treatise (Section VI). Cf. note 289.

[20] Our author here quotes an elegiac stanza from Ovid (*Fasti*, i. 335, 336). The above English translation follows that by Frazer (*Ovid's Fasti*, with an English tr. by Sir James George Frazer [London: Heinemann; New York: Putnam (Loeb Classical Library), 1931], pp. 26, 27). The definitions given by Isidore of Seville may be of analogous interest: "Hostiae apud veteres dicebantur sacrificia quae fiebant antequam ad hostem pergerent. Victimae vero sacrificia quae post victoriam, devictis hostibus, immolabant. Et erant victimae maiora sacrificia quam hostiae. Alii victimam dictam putaverunt, quia ictu percussa cadebat, vel quia vincta ad aras ducebatur." (*Isidori Hispalensis Episcopi Etymologiarum sive Originum libri XX*, ed. W. M. Lindsay, Vol. I [Oxford: Clarendon Press, 1911], VI. xix. 33, 34). These

(3) *Immolare* properly means to offer *molae,* that is, legumes which have been ground *{molitae}* and sprinkled with salt, or even cakes baked from the finest wheat flour. These *molae* always had to be added to the other sacrifices.

4. GERMAN

The German *opfern* originated from the Latin verb "to offer" *{offerre}.*

So much for vocabulary.

C. *Biblical Priesthood and Sacrifice in General*

Now a *sacrifice* in the broad sense is an action instituted by God whereby, in order to honor Him, we ourselves render to Him a particular work which He Himself has commanded. Such sacrifice does in fact honor Him because through it we declare that the One whom we thus worship is truly God and that we are obedient to Him.

Priesthood as a general concept refers to the office of learning and teaching the doctrine which God has handed down, namely, God's Law and the Gospel of Christ; offering to God the sacrifices commanded by Him; and praying for oneself and others — for to this office the promise has been given that God will certainly hear. From this definition it is evident that in the Old Testament church the priests and Levites connected with the Jewish tabernacle did not function merely as butchers responsible for slaughtering beasts and burning the flesh of victims on the altar or concern themselves only with sacrifices. On the contrary, the far greater task intrusted to them, and their first and foremost duty, was to study, preserve, and interpret the true doctrine of God. Specifically, they were to expound to the people the Law of God and the promises concerning Christ; rightly interpret the sacrifices as types and representations of the sacrifice of Messiah (by which alone the sins of the human race would be expiated); explain the services of discipline and gratitude owed to God and the ministry; and learn and disseminate all the skills necessary for elucidating heavenly doctrine and guiding the church. They had to maintain a continuous record

statements of Isidore were taken over almost verbatim by Rabanus Maurus in his medieval encyclopedia, the *De universo,* v. 10 (text in J.-P. Migne, ed., *Patrologiae cursus completus . . . series Latina,* III [Paris, 1864], col. 130).

of the church's history and activities; reckon the year, construct calendars, and determine the times for festivals by observing the movements of sun and moon; and also preserve the arts of medicine, music, and the like. The weightiest responsibility of the priestly college was to judge all doctrinal controversies from God's Word in a pious and clear way. This first and foremost task of the priests — that of guarding and disseminating the heavenly doctrine of God's Law and of the promises concerning Christ — should be considered particularly with reference to the history of the Levitical priesthood. Note Malachi 2:7: "The priest's lips keep knowledge, and they shall seek God's doctrine at his mouth; for he is the messenger of the Lord of hosts." [21]

The second main function of all priests, let it be understood, is to call upon God, pray for themselves and others, and believe assuredly that they are heard for the sake of Christ the Mediator — according to the promise: "Whatever ye shall ask of the Father in My name, He will give it you." [22] Lev. 16 teaches that the priest should pray for himself and for his household and for all the

---

[21] The Lat. uses indicative verbs ("keep" and "shall seek") to render the Heb. imperfects in this verse (יְבַקְשׁוּ and יִשְׁמְרוּ); this is not impossible, but the AV translation ("should keep," "should seek") is contextually preferable. As for our author's phrase, "the history of the Levitical priesthood," and his general treatment of the Levites throughout this work, it is well to remind ourselves that, since he lived prior to the advent of OT documentary criticism (cf. E. G. Kraeling, *The Old Testament Since the Reformation* [New York: Harper, 1955]), he necessarily views the Levitical priesthood largely as a static institution — as it appears in P. This certainly does not vitiate his theological interpretations, but it is a fact worth noting. Of the older and newer approaches, G. B. Gray writes: "According to the one reading of the history, the Levitical priesthood, so far as that term may in that case be appropriately used at all, is applicable to the Jewish priesthood at all periods: i. e., the Jewish priesthood was Levitical in the same sense from its institution onwards. In the other reading, too, the priesthood was Levitical, in one sense or another, for the larger part of Hebrew history, but Levitical at different periods in very different senses. . . . Thus we find in the earliest periods of Hebrew history a wider than the Levitical priesthood: we find this wider priesthood narrowed down by the close of the seventh century to a Levitical priesthood, and still further narrowed from the sixth or fifth centuries to a priesthood within but by no means co-extensive with Levi" (*Sacrifice in the Old Testament* [Oxford: Clarendon Press, 1925], pp. 239, 241).

[22] John 15:16; cf. 14:13, 14.

congregation of Israel.[23] And Lev. 4 states that the priest shall plead for the sinner and for his sin, and it shall be forgiven him.[24]

The priests' third duty is to offer such moral and ceremonial sacrifices as have been established at various times. Heb. 8:3: "Every priest is ordained to offer gifts and sacrifices."[25] 1 Peter 2:5: "Ye are an holy priesthood to offer up spiritual sacrifices acceptable to God by Jesus Christ."

To these three priestly functions stated in the Mosaic law, a fourth was added for the priests of the tribe of Levi: the duty of judging between clean and unclean persons, foods, houses, marriages, etc. And because these last two responsibilities of the tribe of Levi (viz., sacrifices and the discrimination of the clean from the unclean) are particularly described in the third book of Moses, the Septuagint translators gave it the title "Leviticus."

Now there are different *kinds of sacrifices*. Some, namely the Levitical or Mosaic sacrifices in the Old Testament, are considered types or shadows. Others, that is to say the sacrifices of the New Testament, are not shadows but the very things which the shadows represented. And of these latter, one — the obedience of Christ in His passion and death — is a propitiation, because it merits the remission of sins for others and by its great worth placates God's wrath and renders Him propitious. Still other sacrifices are εὐχαριστικά [eucharistic];[26] these do not merit the remission of sins for us or for others but are only testimonies of obedience and gratitude. We shall discuss in detail first the Levitical sacrifices and then priesthood and sacrifice in the New Testament (i. e., that of Christ and of Christians).

23 See especially Lev. 16:6, 11, 17, 24, 33. Strictly speaking, the Heb. refers to "making an atonement" (כִּפֶּר) rather than "praying." The latter translation derives from the Vulgate.

24 See particularly Lev. 4:20, 26, 31, 35. Again, the Heb. actually speaks of "making an atonement," though prayer for the sinner was not foreign to such "coverings over of sin" (this A. Maillot effectively points out in J.-J. von Allmen's *Vocabulary of the Bible,* trans. P. J. Allcock et al. [London: Lutterworth Press, 1958], p. 331).

25 Gk. and AV have "high priest" in this verse.

26 See below, notes 236 and 289.

II
OLD TESTAMENT SACRIFICE

A. The Particular Sacrifices of the Old Testament

The Levitical sacrifices were offerings of animals, foods, wine, produce, etc., commanded by God through Moses; they were to constitute a training ground in obedience owed to God, an energizing force for the public ministry, and types representative of the future sacrifice of Christ and of all spiritual sacrifices acceptable to God through Christ. Twelve varieties of Levitical sacrifices can be noted and distinguished in reading the books of Moses.

1. THE WHOLE BURNT OFFERING

The holocaust sacrifice is so designated because the whole of it was burned on the altar (Lev. 1; 6:8-13).[27] In Hebrew the word is עֹלָה ('ōlāh),[28] from עָלָה {'ālāh}, "it has ascended," for the whole sacrifice on the altar ascends or is consumed — das gar aufgeht.[29] The Greek is ὁλόκαυστον and ὁλοκαύτωμα (or ὁλοκάρπωσις and κάρπωμα,[30] because the entire sacrifice was, one might say, fruit or food for the fire).

One kind of holocaust is the perennial sacrifice, the ὁλοκαύτωμα ἐνδελεχές or עֹלַת תָּמִיד ('ōlath tāmîdh),[28] that is, "continual whole burnt offering," which was to be repeated daily. For every day, both in the morning and in the evening, a lamb had to be offered to God (Num. 28:3-8). This perpetual sacrifice of a lamb is

---

[27] Lev. 6:1-7 in the Vulgate and the AV is numbered as Lev. 5:20-26 in the Heb. Bible and in the Septuagint (ed. Rahlfs), and the remaining verses in chap. 6 are advanced in number accordingly. Here as elsewhere we follow the numeration of the English Bible.

[28] Chytraeus' plena ḥōlem has been changed to defectiva here.

[29] Throughout the translation, German orthography and constructions have been modernized.

[30] From καρπός, "fruit."

interpreted by Peter in 1 Peter 1:18, 19 [31] ("Ye were redeemed with the precious blood of Christ, a Lamb without blemish"), and by John the Baptist ("Behold the Lamb of God, which taketh away the sins of the world").[32] And in Rev. 13:8 Christ is called "the Lamb slain from the foundation of the world." Indeed, all sacrifices of lambs offered to God from the beginning of the world signified that Christ's unique sacrifice forever perfects those being sanctified; as the Psalm says: "Thou art a Priest forever after the order of Melchizedek." [33]

2. THE SIN OFFERING

The sacrifice for sin (specifically of ignorance and omission), Lev. 4; 5:6-13; 6:24-30, appears in the Hebrew as חַטָּאת {ḥaṭṭāth}, from חָטָא {ḥāṭā}, "he has sinned," and חִטֵּא {ḥiṭṭē}, "he has expiated sin." [34] The Septuagint translates it περὶ ἁμαρτίας in Ps. 40:6,[35] thus: וַחֲטָאָה[36] לֹא שָׁאָלְתָּ עוֹלָה, ὁλοκαυτώματα καὶ περὶ ἁμαρτίας οὐκ ἐζήτησας [37] ("Burnt offering and sin offering hast Thou not required"). Paul has retained this expression in Rom. 8:3: περὶ ἁμαρτίας κατέκρινεν τὴν ἁμαρτίαν ἐν τῇ σαρκί [38] (God

31 The text reference here is wrongly given as 1 Peter 4; this (printer's?) error has been corrected in the translation.

32 John 1:29.

33 Ps. 110:4; quoted in Heb. 5:6; 7:17, 21 (cf. Heb. 6:20—7:28).

34 "This offering, as its name implies, had a closer relation to sin and its expiation than either the burnt-offering or the peace-offering. Even so, the only sins for which it could atone were those committed in ignorance (RV, 'unwittingly'). . . . It should be explained that in a community which gave great prominence to the due performance of a complicated ritual, and laid the main emphasis upon actions themselves rather than upon their underlying motives, it was easy to sin 'unwittingly.' . . . All the OT evidence appears to indicate that it was not until post-exilic times that the sin-offering came into prominence, the usual offerings in pre-exilic times being the burnt-offering and the peace-offering." (C. R. North, in *A Theological Word Book of the Bible,* ed. Alan Richardson [New York: Macmillan, 1950], p. 207)

35 Psalm numeration, here as elsewhere, follows the AV.

36 In this word the misprinted מ (m) has been corrected to ח (ḥ). This noun is cognate with חַטָּאת and has the same meaning; it has been conjectured that the latter should be read here (K 1009).

37 This Septuagint reading follows Codex Alexandrinus (see R, II, 41).

38 The erroneous form σαρκῇ has been corrected to σαρκί here.

condemned or destroyed the sin clinging to our flesh, in that Christ for a sin offering, or as a victim, bore the guilt and penalty for sin).[39] Cf. Hos. 4:8, where we read that the priests "eat up the sins of my people," that is, eat the victims or beasts offered for sin.

There were two varieties of sin offering. For the priests were allowed to eat the meat of those sacrificial animals whose blood was not brought into the tabernacle of the testimony (Lev. 6[g] and 10). But the skin, flesh, head, etc., of the animals whose blood was taken into the sanctuary were burned outside the camp, and the priests were not permitted to use any part for food (Lev. 4; Heb. 13). "For the bodies of those beasts, whose blood is brought into the sanctuary by the high priest for a sin offering, are to be[h] burned without the camp. Wherefore Jesus also, that He might sanctify the people with His own blood, suffered without the gate. Let us go forth therefore unto Him without the camp, bearing His reproach. For here have we no continuing city." [40]

3. THE TRESPASS OFFERING

The sacrifice for a trespass — for a sin committed ἐκ προαιρέσεως (deliberately and of one's own free will), Lev. 5:1-7, 14-19; 6:1-7,[41] is expressed in Hebrew by the word אָשָׁם {'āshām},

[39] "God sent His Son . . . περὶ ἁμαρτίας. These words indicate the aim of the mission. Christ was sent in our nature 'in connection with sin.' The RV renders 'as an offering for sin.' This is legitimate, for περὶ ἁμαρτίας is used both in the LXX (Lev. iv. 33 and passim, Ps. xl. 6, 2 Chr. xxix. 24) and in the NT (Heb. x. 6, 8) in the sense of 'sin-offering' (usually answering to Heb. חַטָּאת, but in Isa. liii. 10 to אָשָׁם); but it is not formally necessary. But when the question is asked, In what sense did God send His Son 'in connection with sin'? there is only one answer possible. He sent Him to expiate sin by His sacrificial death. This is the centre and foundation of Paul's gospel (iii. 25 ff.), and to ignore it here is really to assume that he used the words καὶ περὶ ἁμαρτίας (which have at least sacrificial associations) either with no meaning in particular, or with a meaning alien to his constant and dearest thoughts" (James Denney, in EG II, 645). C. F. D. Moule gives a similar interpretation of the prepositional phrase (An Idiom Book of New Testament Greek [Cambridge: University Press, 1953], p. 63). Cf. Section II. C. (3) below.

[40] Heb. 13:11-14. The Vulgate is followed exactly except that crementur ("are to be burned") is substituted for cremantur ("are burned").

[41] See above, note 27.

which means both "trespass," and "trespass offering" or "propitiatory sacrifice."[42] The significance of this sacrifice is explained by Isaiah (53:10): אִם־תָּשִׂים אָשָׁם נַפְשׁוֹ יִרְאֶה זֶרַע ("When He[43] shall make His soul a trespass" — i. e., a trespass offering — "He shall see His seed, He shall prolong His days"[44]); and by Paul (2 Cor. 5:21): "God hath made Christ to be sin" (i. e., a victim expiating sin) "for us, who knew no sin, that we might be made the righteousness of God in Him."

4. THE MEAL OFFERING

מִנְחָה (minḥāh) means "gift," or "meal offering" of inanimate substances such as the finest wheat flour, high quality meal, bread, legumes, salt, wine, olive oil, etc.; this offering was to be added to all the whole burnt offerings and to every kind of animal sacrifice (Lev. 2; 6:14-23; Num. 15; 28; 29 passim).[45] Latin uses the terms "sacrificial cake" {fertum}, "immolation" ({immolatio}, from molae [legumes ground and sprinkled with salt]), "libation" ({libatio}, from libum, a kind of cake[46]), "wheat offering" {adoreum sacrificium}, and "wheat cake" {farreum}.

Three varieties of meal offering are distinguished. First was that consisting of the finest uncooked wheat flour. Second were offerings of loaves or cakes cooked either in an oven or in a pan or on a platter. Third were sacrifices of ears of corn taken from the first fruits, dried by fire, and laid in oil and frankincense.

[42] "This offering seems to have been confined to offenses against God or man that could be estimated and so covered by compensation. . . . The trespass-offering is unknown to JED and the older Hebrew literature. . . . The Messianic servant offers himself as an אָשָׁם in compensation for the sins of the people, interposing for them as their substitute — Is. 53:10 (incorrectly, offering for sin, AV, RV)." (BDB 79, 80)

[43] Heb. has "Thou."

[44] It will be seen that the Heb. quoted by our author stops short of this last clause.

[45] See above, note 9 and the corresponding text.

[46] Libatio and libum derive from libo (√ LIQV-), "take a little of/sip/ make a drink offering/offer." Ovid (Fasti, iii. 733, 734) relates the words for "libation" and "cake" to the god Liber, an Italian deity of planting and agriculture who was later identified with Bacchus; Liber likewise has the root LIQV-. Cf. note 20.

5. THE PEACE OFFERING

The peace offering, or eucharistic sacrifice (as Luther renders it by *Dankopfer*), Lev. 3; 7:11-21, 28-34; 10:14, appears in Hebrew as[1] זֶבַח שְׁלָמִים *{zebhaḥ sheʾlāmîm}*, from שָׁלֵם *{shālēm}*, "it was complete." This verb gives us שָׁלוֹם *{shālôm}*,[47] "completeness/peace/safety/salvation." The Greek for the peace offering is thus ϑυσία σωτηρίου, "saving sacrifice"; and the Latin, "peace offering" *{hostia pacificorum}*, or testimony of gratitude for peace and salvation received from God. Others have translated it "retributive sacrifice" *{sacrificium retributionum}* by deriving it from שִׁלֵּם *{shillēm}*, which means "retribution/recompense."[48]

6. THE THANK OFFERING

A sacrifice related to[49] the peace offering is the sacrifice of praise or thanksgiving (זֶבַח תּוֹדָה *{zebhaḥ tôdhāh}*, ϑυσία αἰνέσεως), Lev. 7:12, 13, 15. It was similar to the *minḥāh* or meal offering; it was always to be combined with the peace offering, in which cattle, sheep, and goats were sacrificed. By presenting a thank offering, the faithful acknowledged that they had received blessing from God and therefore that they in turn praised and worshiped God as the source of the blessing.

The prophets and apostles very frequently mention this sacrifice of praise. Heb. 13:15: "Through Christ we are offering[50] the

[47] Here written in the more common *plena* form; Chytraeus gives the less common *(defectiva)* spelling שָׁלֹם.

[48] "The Heb. word for this offering (in early times often called *zebah*, 'sacrifice,' 'slaughter' simply) is *shelem*. It is translated 'peace-offering' in the EVV [i. e., AV and RV] because of its obvious relation to the word *shalom* (peace), as of an offering that promoted peaceful relations with God. It may, however, in some passages equally well be rendered 'recompense-offering,' and this is supported by the fact that the three classes of *shelem* (thank-offering, votive-offering, and freewill-offering; cf. Lev. 7:11-16, 22:21) are clearly in the nature of recognitions of benefits received or expected. . . . Of all the sacrifices the peace-offering retains most clearly the characteristics of the ancient communion sacrifice, since God and the worshipper were thought to share a common meal." (C. R. North, in *A Theological Word Book of the Bible*, ed. Alan Richardson [New York: Macmillan, 1950], p. 207)

[49] "A division of זֶבַח הַשְּׁלָמִים" (BDB 392).

[50] The Gk. and AV have "let us offer."

sacrifice of praise to God continually, that is, the fruit of our lips giving thanks to His name." Ps. 50:14, 15, 23: "Offer unto God the sacrifice of praise; and call upon Me in the day of trouble and I will deliver thee, and thou shalt glorify Me. The thank offering [51] shall glorify Me." Ps. 116:17: "I will offer to Thee the sacrifice of thanksgiving and will call upon the name of the Lord." 2 Chron. 29:31: "Offer sacrifices and praises in the house [52] of the Lord." [53] Jonah 2:9: "I will sacrifice unto Thee with the voice of thanksgiving."

7. THE OFFERING OF FIRST FRUITS

The offering of the first fruits and first-born, instructions for which are given in Ex. 13:1, 2, 11-16; 23:16, 19; Lev. 2:12, 14; 23:10, 17, 20; Deut. 26:1-11,ʲ and elsewhere, is represented by the Hebrew בְּכֹרוֹת (beₖhōrôth) [54] and רֵאשִׁית {rē'shîth}, and by the Greek ἀπαρχαί and πρωτογεννήματα. Five varieties are distinguished in the Mosaic writings: (1) Standing crops,[55] or first fruits of all new produce grown on the land, Deut. 26:1-11.ᵏ Pliny speaks of this kind of offering in Bk. XVIII: "And people were not even accustomed to taste the produce of a new harvest or vintage [56] before the priests had offered a libation of the firstfruits." (2) Ears of corn in bundles, Lev. 23:10. (3) Kernels of corn beaten out of green ears which had not yet been ground into meal, Lev. 2:12, 14. (4) Bread made from two tenths of the finest

---

[51] Heb. has "The offerer of praise."

[52] *Dono* is misprinted for *domo* in the text here.

[53] The Heb. reads: "Bring sacrifices and thank offerings into the house of the Lord."

[54] This is a plural form of בְּכוֹר, "first-born"; in many of the passages cited here by Chytraeus the cognate noun בִּכּוּרִים, "first fruits," is employed. These two nouns can have the same consonantal pattern in the construct plural.

[55] Reading *novalia* for the misprint *novatia*.

[56] The text has *vicia* misprinted for *vina*. The quotation is taken from the elder Pliny's *Natural History*, XVIII. ii. 8, where Pliny (A. D. 23—79) is discoursing on Roman agricultural practices during the period of Rome's founding and the early monarchy. See *Pliny: Natural History*, with an English tr. by H. Rackham, V (Cambridge: Harvard University Press [Loeb Classical Library], 1950), 194, 195.

leavened wheat flour; this sacrifice was offered on the day of Pentecost, Lev. 23:17, 20. (5) Victuals or foods, Num. 15:20, 21.[57] In general (6), firstfruits and firstlings which were to be offered to God in accordance with the instructions in Ex. 13:1, 2, 11-16;[58] 22:29, 30; 23:16, 19; Deut. 12:6, 17; Ezek. 20:40.[59]

8. THE OFFERING OF TITHES

There were four kinds of tithes: (1) the δεκάς or tenth of all produce and animals; this the people owed to the tribe of Levites for the preservation of the ministry and the support of its ministers, Lev. 27:30-33;[60] Num. 18:21, 24; Deut. 14:22-27. (2) The Levites gave to the priests tithes of the tithes which they received from the people. These were called δευτεροδέκαδαι,[61] Num. 18:26, 28. (3)[1] Special tithes were set aside by individuals and used by them for traveling expenses when they went up to Jerusalem each year.[62] (4) Also, every third year tithes were collected in a common chest so that alms might be given to the poor, Deut. 14:28, 29; 26:12-15; Tobit 1:6-8. In Bk. XIV of his Com-

[57] The Lat. words employed here *(cibi, pulmenta)* are found in the Vulgate of Num. 15:20, 21. The Heb. speaks of cakes made from new meal dough.

[58] The text incorrectly has Ex. 3 for Ex. 13 here; this is probably a printer's error.

[59] The text incorrectly has Ezek. 25. Probably Ezek. 20 is meant; cf. also Ezek. 44:30; 48:14.

[60] This key passage concludes the book of Leviticus.

[61] Chytraeus incorrectly accents this word paroxytone; the correct (proparoxytone) accent has been substituted. Possibly the error is due to a confusion between the two nouns for tithe: δεκάς, -άδος (a third-declension noun), and δεκάδη — or better δεκάτη (a first-declension noun from the adjective δέκατος).

[62] This is based on Tobit 1:7, which, to be precise, speaks of a tithe which was spent at Jerusalem rather than expended in traveling there. The full passage (1:6-8) reads (AV): "But I alone went often to Jerusalem at the feasts, as it was ordained unto all the people of Israel by an everlasting decree, having the firstfruits and tenths of increase, with that which was first shorn; and them gave I at the altar to the priests the children of Aaron. The first tenth part of all increase I gave to the sons of Aaron, who ministered at Jerusalem: another tenth part I sold away, and went, and spent it every year at Jerusalem: And the third I gave unto them to whom it was meet, as Debora my father's mother had commanded me, because I was left an orphan by my father." According to R. H. Pfeiffer, the apocryphal book of Tobit was written shortly after 200 B. C.

mentary on Ezekiel, Jerome writes that these tithes were called πτωχοδέκαδαι, and at the same time informs us that the priests were not allowed to exact from the people in the name of tithes more than a sixtieth of the produce of the land.[63]

9. THE SACRIFICE OF A RAM IN THE CONSECRATION OF THE PRIESTS, LEV. 8:22-34

10. THE OFFERING OF A GOAT AND A BULL CALF AT THE FEAST OF EXPIATION

This took place on the tenth day of the seventh month and is described in Lev. 16. It is interpreted in the Epistle to the Hebrews, 9:11, 12: "Christ being come an high priest of good

[63] In discussing Jewish tithes, Jerome writes: "There were, moreover, other tithes, which they laid up for the poor; in Greek these are called πτωχο-δέκαδαι [poor tithes]. However, the firstfruits which were offered from produce were not in fact specified as to particular amount, but were left entirely to the judgment of the offerers. We have heard a tradition, not prescribed by a law of the Hebrews, but well established by the rabbis' authority, that one gave the priests at most a fortieth part, and at least a sixtieth; between these limits one was allowed to offer whatever he wished. Therefore what in the Pentateuch was left completely indefinite, is here [Ezekiel 45:13] specifically defined on account of the avarice of the priests, lest they should exact more from the people in taking the firstfruits; that is, the people are to offer a sixtieth part of the produce of the land" (my tr. from Jerome's *Commentaria in Ezechielem*, Bk. XIV, in Migne, op. cit., XXV [Paris, 1884], col. 451). Concerning this "poor tithe" we read in A. R. Fausset's *Bible Encyclopaedia and Dictionary* (Grand Rapids: Zondervan, n. d.), p. 693: "Tobit (i. 7, 8) says he gave a third tithe to the poor; Josephus (Ant. iv. 8, 8, para. 22) also mentions a third tithe; so Jerome too on Ezek. xlv. Maimonides denies a third tithe (which would be an excessive burden) and represents the second tithe [i. e., Chytraeus' tithe no. 3] of the third and sixth years as shared between the poor and the Levites. . . . Ewald suggests that for two years the tithe was virtually voluntary, on the third year compulsory. Thus there was a yearly tithe for the Levites, a second yearly tithe for two years for the festivals; but this second tithe on every third year was shared by the Levites with the poor." This latter (Talmudic) interpretation is thus described in *Harper's Bible Dictionary*, ed. M. S. and J. L. Miller, 4th ed. (New York, 1956), p. 765: The rabbis supposed "two separate tithes to be presented every year. The first was to be given to the Levites; the second was to be expended in feasts at Jerusalem, except in the 3d and 6th years of the Sabbatical cycle of seven (Amos 4:4), when it was designated for the poor." For an orthodox Graf-Wellhausen view of the tithe problem in the OT, see A. S. Peake's article "Tithe," in Hastings' *Dictionary of the Bible*, IV (New York: Scribner, 1911), 780, 781.

things to come, by a greater and more perfect tabernacle, not made with hands; neither by the blood of goats and calves, but by His own blood He entered in once into the holy place and obtained eternal redemption for us"; and also in Hebrews 10:4-7, 10:[64] "It is not possible that the blood of bulls and of goats should take away sins. Wherefore when He cometh into the world, He saith, Sacrifice and offering Thou wouldest not, but a body hast Thou prepared Me; in burnt offerings and sacrifices for sin Thou hast had no pleasure. Then said I, Lo, I come (in the volume of the book it is written of Me) to do Thy will, O God. By this will we are sanctified through the offering of the body of Jesus Christ once for all."

11. THE OFFERING OF A RED HEIFER

The heifer's ashes were sprinkled for [m] lustral water, Num. 19. "If the blood of bulls and of goats and the ashes of an heifer sprinkling the unclean sanctifieth to the purifying of the flesh, how much more shall the blood of Christ, who through the eternal Spirit offered Himself without spot to God, purge our [65] conscience from dead works to serve the living God." [66]

12. THE SACRIFICE OF A LAMB AT THE PASSOVER

The significance of this offering is explained by Paul in 1 Cor. 5:7: "Christ our Passover is sacrificed for us."

*　　*　　*

Some divide these twelve kinds of sacrifice into two groups. First there are the holy of holy — or most holy — sacrifices, which

[64] Which quotes Ps. 40:6-8, where the Septuagint offers to some extent "a free, generalizing rendering" of the Heb. (Franz Delitzsch, *Biblical Commentary on the Psalms,* trans. David Eaton, II [London: Hodder and Stoughton, 1888], 45 — *q. v.*).

[65] AV has "your"; Chytraeus' reading ("our") has stronger textual support.

[66] Heb. 9:13, 14. G. B. Gray writes: "It has sometimes been discussed whether the red cow, the ashes of which were used as an ingredient in the liquid prepared and used for the removal of uncleanness incurred by contact with the dead, was a sacrifice or not. . . . We may say . . . that the red cow differed from sacrifices in one substantial point alone: they were gifts at the altar, it was not" (*Sacrifice in the Old Testament,* p. 31). It is worthwhile noting that Gray devotes the final four chapters (xxii—xxv) of his work to the next and last sacrifice in Chytraeus' enumeration: the Passover victim.

particularly represented the propitiatory sacrifice of Christ; they alone were immolated on the north side of the altar, and either they were burned completely or no one but the priests were allowed to eat of them. Such were the whole burnt offering, the sin offering, the trespass offering, etc. Second there are the sacrifices of average holiness, of which the people or the family performing the sacrifice were permitted to eat — e. g., the peace offering, the thank offering, the sacrifice of the paschal lamb, etc. He who wishes to employ this distinction, such as it is, may do so.

God instituted so many different kinds of sacrifice in order that the Israelites might continue to fear[n] the Word which He delivered to them and not, like the neighboring peoples, choose their religious activities and worship in accord with personal preference but observe only the sacrifices set down in the Law. Moreover, the variety of Christ's benefits and of spiritual sacrifices were foreshadowed by this diversity of sacrificial types. At the same time an indication was given that the Levitical sacrifices, because of their great variety and multiplicity and because they were repeated so often, did not expiate sins or perfect those who offered them, i. e., did not impart to the sacrificers a perfect and complete liberation from sin or true and perfect righteousness; but they were shadows of Christ's body, offered once for all for us on the altar of the cross, as Hebrews 10:1-14 says:[67] "For the Law, having a shadow of good things to come and not the very image of the things, can never with those sacrifices which they offered continually year by year make the comers thereunto perfect. For then would they not have ceased to be offered? Because that the worshipers once purged should have had no more conscience of sins. But in those sacrifices there is a remembrance made of sins every year. For it is not possible that the blood of bulls and of goats should take away sins. Wherefore when He cometh into the world, He saith, Sacrifice and offering Thou wouldest not, but a body hast Thou prepared Me; in burnt offerings and sacrifices for sin Thou hast had no pleasure. Then said I, Lo, I come (in the volume of the book it is written of Me) to do Thy will, O God. Above when He said, Sacrifice and offering and burnt offerings and offering for sin Thou wouldest not, neither hadst pleasure therein, which are

[67] See above, note 64.

offered by the Law, then said I,[68] Lo, I come to do Thy will, O God.
He taketh away the first that He may establish the second. By the
which will we are sanctified through the offering of the body of
Jesus Christ, accomplished once for all. And every priest standeth
daily ministering and offering oftentimes the same sacrifices, which
can never take away sins; but this Man, after He had offered one
sacrifice for sins, forever [69] sat down on the right hand of God;
from henceforth expecting till His enemies be made His footstool.
For by one offering He hath perfected forever them that are being
sanctified." °

B. *An Anatomy of Old Testament Sacrifice*

The *efficient cause* [70] of the sacrificial system — the ordainer
and establisher of it — is the Lord God Himself, who by His
express word commands the several kinds of offerings. Thus again

[68] The Gk. has "He."

[69] The AV construes "forever" with the previous "offered"; that Chytraeus'
rendering is the correct one is evident from Marcus Dods' statements in
EG IV, 345: "εἰς τὸ διηνεκὲς cannot be construed with προσενέγκας but
must be taken with ἐκάθισεν. 'To say of the Levitical priests that they
προσθέρουσιν εἰς τὸ διηνεκὲς (ver. 1) is appropriate; to say of Christ that
He προσήνεγκεν εἰς τὸ διην. is almost a self-contradiction' (Vaughan).
εἰς τὸ διηνεκὲς ἐκάθισεν balances ἕστηκεν καθ' ἡμέραν, and cf. especially i. 3."

[70] "An agent; that which by its activity or its exercise of power produces
existence or change in another" (Bernard Wuellner, *Dictionary of Scholastic
Philosophy* [Milwaukee: Bruce, 1956], p. 39). On the modified scholastic
methodology of Lutheran scholars of the Reformation-Orthodoxy period,
see especially Max Wundt, *Die deutsche Schulmetaphysik des 17. Jahrhunderts* (Tübingen: Mohr, 1939 [Heidelberger Abhandlungen zur Philosophie und ihrer Geschichte, 29]), and the following three works by
(Hans) Emil Weber: *Die philosophische Scholastik des deutschen Protestantismus im Zeitalter der Orthodoxie* (Leipzig: Quelle & Meyer, 1907
[Abhandlungen zur Philosophie und ihrer Geschichte, 1]); *Der Einfluss
der protestantischen Schulphilosophie auf die orthodox-lutherische Dogmatik*
(Leipzig: A. Deichert, 1908); *Reformation, Orthodoxie und Rationalismus*
(Gütersloh: C. Bertelsmann, 1937—51 [Beiträge zur Förderung christlicher
Theologie, II: 35, 51]), 2 vols. It should be stressed, however, that Chytraeus employs only the most general scholastic terms and does so with such
moderation and flexibility that it would be manifestly unfair to place him
in a single category with Quenstedt and the other Lutheran dogmaticians
of the next century. Chytraeus is primarily an exegete, not a systematician;
and he is far closer to the Reformation — both chronologically and methodologically — than to the period of Orthodoxy.

and again in Leviticus this common προοίμιον [prefatory statement], "The Lord spake unto Moses, saying . . ." is repeated and inculcated — so that we might know that these sacrificial rites, however contemptible and absurd they may [p] seem from the standpoint of human reason, are the product and command of divine wisdom and majesty. Let us also learn from them that no sacrifices and no worship are pleasing and acceptable to God unless God Himself has instituted or commended [71] them by His express word. Deut. 12:32: "What thing I command you, observe to do it only unto the Lord; thou shalt not add thereto nor diminish from it." Deut. 4:2: "Ye shall not add unto the word which I command you, neither shall ye diminish ought from it." Is. 29:13: "In vain they do worship Me, teaching for doctrines the commandments of men." [72] Ezek. 20:19: "Walk in My statutes. . . ." These and similar judgments against the ἐθελοθρησκίαι [self-made religions [73]] of all times should remain before our eyes.

The *material from which* [74] it was permissible to secure sacrificial offerings was either the animals designated for sacrifice by God's express word (such as lambs, bull calves, he-goats, heifers, she-goats, and, among birds, turtledoves, young pigeons, sparrows) or inanimate substances (such as the produce of the land, flour, bread, cakes, wine, olive oil, money, etc.). The sacrifice of human beings to God was prohibited, as at a later time the Israelites and the Gentiles not only immolated people but even sacrificed their own children to Moloch and other idols. As we read in 2 Kings 16:3 and 21:6, Ahaz and Manasseh, kings of Judah, burned their sons in the fire of Gehenna; and examples of human sacrifice are provided by Iphigenia, Menaeceus, Erechtheus' daughter, Macaria, Hercules, Codrus, that poor man of Massilia, Quintus Curtius, and

71 The text has the late form *sancivit* (for *sanxit*); see SGLL 363, and cf. note 138 below.

72 Our author's translation of Is. 29:13, like the renderings in Matt. 15:9 and Mark 7:7, is based on the Septuagint text of the verse.

73 Perhaps "would-be religions" (A-G 217). The compound is a Christian formation and appears only in Col. 2:23.

74 *Materia ex qua,* "'the matter from which,' i. e. . . . that from which something arises or of which it consists or the material or the material cause of a thing, the same as *causa materialis*" (D-B 669).

others.[75] It is understandable that such sacrifices appeared, for Noah's posterity had [q] heard that a Christ-man was to come who

[75] *Iphigenia* was "in mythology a daughter of Agamemnon. For some reason he was obliged to sacrifice her, either because he had vowed to sacrifice the fairest thing born in a particular year, and she was born then, or because he had offended Artemis by an impious boast" (OCD 457). The sacrifice of her is referred to by Kierkegaard at several places in *Fear and Trembling*. *Menaeceus* (better, Menoeceus), a mythological figure, killed himself when he learned that Thebes could not survive an attack of the Seven without an atonement for the killing of a dragon; that the victim had to be one of the Sparti and unmarried; and that no one else fulfilled these requisites (OCD 558). "The chief legend of *Erechtheus* concerns his daughters, of whom there were three. . . . When Eumolpus . . . invaded Attica, Erechtheus inquired of Delphi how he might win the victory. He was told that he should do so if he sacrificed one of his daughters. Chthonia, therefore, was sacrificed by consent of her mother Praxithea, probably by her own also. . . . The other daughters killed themselves" (OCD 337). By *Macaria* Chytraeus certainly means Macareus, a son of Lycaon. According to one tradition, when Zeus came to visit King Lycaon, he tempted his divine guest by killing and serving to him one of his sons to eat; Macareus, however, is not named as the son who was sacrificed. For the various and conflicting accounts, see J. G. Frazer's detailed note in Vol. I, pp. 390—393 of his edition of Apollodorus' *Library* (London: Heinemann; New York: Putnam [Loeb Classical Library], 1921). The faulty spelling "Macaria" is probably explained by the fact that in Apollodorus' list of the sons of Lycaon, the name Macareus appears in the accusative case (Μαχαρέα, transliterated "Macarea") — see *The Library*, III. viii. 1. Apollodorus describes the death of *Hercules* thus: He "proceeded to Mount Oeta, in the Trachinian territory, and there constructed a pyre, mounted it and gave orders to kindle it. . . . While the pyre was burning, it is said that a cloud passed under Hercules and with a peal of thunder wafted him up to heaven" (ibid., II. vii. 7, Frazer's tr.). The sacrifice of *Codrus*, an early king of Athens, is set forth in the following legendary terms: "When Attica was invaded by the Dorian Heraclids, who had heard from Delphi that they would be victorious if Codrus' life were spared, a friendly Delphian informed the Athenians of this oracle. Codrus thereupon went forth in woodcutter's garb, invited death by starting a quarrel with Dorian warriors, and so saved his country" (OCD 207). By "that poor man of *Massilia*" Chytraeus refers to a legend concerning ancient Marseilles (Gk., Massalia; Lat., Massilia) which is given by Servius (a fourth-century commentator on Vergil), who claims to have derived it from Petronius: "At Marseilles, whenever an epidemic struck, one of the poor citizens offered himself, and the city was obliged to feed him on ritual dishes at its expense for a whole year. At the end of this time, he was crowned with laurels, dressed in sacred attire, and accompanied by imprecations that all the city's evils fall on him, was led through the entire city and then drowned" (*Ad Aeneid*, iii. 57; my translation). After a careful analysis of the tradition Michel Clerc, the foremost

would take the sins of others upon Himself and expiate them by His own death.[76]

The *material* structure *in which* (if I may so designate it),[77] or the place where, sacrifices were alone permitted to be offered to God was the tabernacle of the testimony — *die Stiftskirche*.[78] For [1] God wanted the Israelites to be ruled, both in their conception of Him and in their divine worship, solely by the Word which He delivered to them and not to choose ceremonials or places of sacrifice by personal preference.[79] Therefore He bound them to one tabernacle or temple, in order that [2] the ministry might be preserved in a particular public place and so that [3] they might be admonished to maintain the unity of true doctrine and faith and not depart from the true God and from His Word and the worship ordained by Him, thereby falling into error and idolatry at the first occasion. For where individuals are allowed to establish private religious get-togethers and conventicles, it is evident that the unanimity and purity of doctrine are easily corrupted and destroyed, and the ministry and public meetings simply put to rout. At the same time God wished to indicate by this law that [4] only in the true church, which is the tabernacle and temple of God, and

authority on the ancient history of Marseilles, rejects it on several grounds, and asks in conclusion: "Comment se fait-il que, pour Marseille, ce fait si curieux ait échappé à l'amateur d'anecdotes de ce genre qu'était Valère-Maxime?" (*Massalia*, I [Marseilles: Tacussel, 1927], 456). *Quintus Curtius* is erroneously given for Manius (or Marcus) Curtius, a brave young knight and hero of an aetiological myth, who, in obedience to an oracle and in order to save his country, plunged armed and on horseback into a chasm which suddenly opened in the Roman Forum (OCD 246).

76 Chytraeus is of course not trying here to justify human sacrifice among pagan peoples; he is rather arguing that the universal need for atonement has led men to attempt their own human sacrifices apart from God's promise and plan to provide a once-for-all sacrifice for sin.

77 Chytraeus asks leave of his readers to use the expression *materia in qua* in a nontechnical way. In scholastic parlance the phrase designated "that in which an action and the corresponding faculty has its bearer and possessor, or the subject of an action and of the faculty belonging to it" (D-B 669).

78 In modern German this word means "collegiate church," and *Stiftshütte* is used for the tabernacle.

79 Contrast the principle accepted axiomatically by many Americans today that each individual should "join a church" which best satisfies his personal psychological and social needs. Cf. note 109.

by a faith which illumines the way before the High Priest [80] of the church, Jesus Christ, might sacrifices and worship pleasing to God be offered.

For these four reasons, God requires with great sternness that victims be offered to Him at the door of the tabernacle and nowhere else. Lev. 17:3, 4, 8, 9: "Whatsoever man bringeth not his sacrifice to the Lord unto the door of the tabernacle shall be cut off from among his people." And often God reiterates this judgment (Deut. 12:13, 14, 32): "Take heed to thyself that thou offer not thy burnt offerings in every place that thou seest; but in the place which the Lord your God shall choose, there ye shall come and offer in that place your victims. What thing I command you, observe to do it only unto the Lord; thou shalt not add thereto nor diminish from it." Hence even Plato sets forth a law (Bk. X) which he perhaps received from the ancient fathers: "Let this be the simple form of the law: No man shall have sacred rites in a private house. When he would sacrifice, let him go to the temples and hand over his offerings to the priests, who see to the sanctity of such things, and let him pray himself with the priests, and let any one who pleases join with him in prayer." [81]

---

[80] Lat., *summus sacerdos,* lit. "the highest priest," an expression employed from Tertullian on to mean "bishop" (SGLL 360), and by St. Thomas to refer to the pope (D-B 982). Biblically, as equivalent to ἀρχιερεύς, it signified the Jewish high priest (B-J 368, 369).

[81] Chytraeus gives the Greek text and a Latin translation of this passage from Plato's *Laws,* x. 909. In cases such as this where our author quotes extensively in Greek from a secular author, it has not been thought necessary to reproduce the original text — especially when the Greek author is so well known that editions of his works are readily available. The English translation of the passage is based on Jowett (*The Dialogues of Plato,* trans. B. Jowett, intro. Raphael Demos, II [New York: Random House, 1937], 651). Chytraeus (either intentionally or because his text did not include it) omits "and priestesses" from the clause which in Jowett reads, "let him go to the temples and hand over his offerings to the priests and priestesses"; this is the only significant difference between Chytraeus' text and Jowett's.

Of this passage in the *Laws* George H. Sabine writes (*A History of Political Theory,* rev. ed. [New York: Holt, 1950], pp. 84, 85): "Religion, from the point of view of the *Laws,* must be subject to the regulation and supervision of the state, just as education is. Consequently Plato forbids any kind of private religious exercises and enacts that rites may be performed only in public temples and by authorized priests. In this he is influenced partly by his dislike of certain disorderly forms of religion to which, as he remarks, hysterical persons and especially women are prone, and partly by

The *nature*[82] of sacrifice is expressed in its definition,[83] but the characteristics[84] of individual ceremonial sacrifices, i.e., all the rites and actions which meet the eye, are described at length in the first ten chapters of Leviticus.

There were ten principal *ends* or valid purposes of Levitical sacrifice. [1]ʳ First, the pious offered sacrifices to obey and honor the God who required and approved this worship by His express word; that is, by sacrificing they testified that they acknowledged the One whom they thus worshiped as the only true God and demonstrated that they owed obedience and gratitude to Him. [2] Second, the sacrificial system was the nerve and sinew of the priesthood or ministry of the Jewish church, and the sinew of the public assemblies in which there occurred a general proclamation and transmittal to posterity of the true doctrine concerning God and His Son, our Lord and Redeemer Jesus Christ, who was to be offered as a victim for the entire human race. A parallel thus exists with the Lord's Supper, which in the New Testament is the nerve of the church's public assemblings and of the propagation both of the doctrine of the death of Christ as a victim immolated for our sins and of the teaching that the remission of sins and eternal salvation are assuredly to be given to any individual who in faith flees to Him for refuge.

[3] Beyond that, the sacrifices were principally representations or types of the sacrifice and benefits of Christ which are set forth in the New Testament. For the Levitical sacrifices did not merit the remission of sins, nor did they placate the wrath of God; they were only signs to bring to mind the future sacrifice of Christ, which alone was a λύτρον[85] or ransom for the sins of the human

the feeling that a private religion withdraws men from their allegiance to the state. . . . These proposals are strongly out of keeping with the practice of the Greeks."

82 Lat., *forma* ("form"). *"Forma* is the more specific definiteness that imparts to a subject, in itself indifferent, its characteristic peculiarity; or it is the conception of anything existing in a definite manner." (Luthardt, as trans. in Hay and Jacobs' English ed. of Schmid's *Doctrinal Theology of the Evangelical Lutheran Church,* 5th ed. [Philadelphia: United Lutheran Publication House, 1899], p. 674)

83 Given in section I. C. above.

84 Lat., *formae* ("forms").

85 Occurs in Matt. 20:28, Mark 10:45.

race. Col. 2:17 speaks of this purpose of the sacrificial system when it says that the Mosaic rites were "shadows of things to come, but the body is of Christ." Heb. 10:1 reads: "The Law had a shadow of the good things of eternity,[86] not the very image of the things." Likewise Heb. 8:4, 5: "The Levitical priests that offer gifts according to the Law should serve[87] unto the example and shadow of heavenly things, as Moses received the admonition: See that thou make all things according to the archetype showed to thee in the mount." All these[s] statements with regard to Christ's sacrifice are pertinent, and especially so are the New Testament assertions that the blood of Christ has been shed for the remission of our sins. For all these testimonies at the same time constitute an antithesis to the blood of lambs and of other animals which was shed in the Levitical sacrifices and by which no one was freed from sin or attained to the remission of sins before God — as 1 Peter 1:18, 19 proves: "We were redeemed with the precious blood of Christ, as of a lamb without blemish," not by the blood of a lamb in perennial sacrifice, daily poured out;[88] not by the blood of a lamb offered at the Passover; not by the blood of Abel's lamb;[89] etc. John 1:29: "Behold the Lamb of God, which taketh away the sin of the world." 1 John 1:7: "The blood of Jesus Christ, God's Son," (not the blood of Mosaic sacrifices) "cleanseth us from all sin." Eph. 1:7 and Col. 1:14: "In Christ we have redemption through His blood,[90] the forgiveness of sins." Matt. 26:28: "This is My blood of the new testament, which is shed for all people[91] for the remission of sins." Heb. 10:4, 14 (and cf. Heb. 9): "It is not possible that the blood of bulls and of goats should take away sins," but Christ "by one offering hath perfected forever them that are sanctified."[92]

---

[86] The Gk. and AV have "of good things to come."

[87] The Gk. and AV have simply "serve." *Serviant* may be a misprint for *serviunt.*

[88] See above, section II. A. 1.

[89] Cf. Heb. 12:24.

[90] The phrase "through His blood" appears in the original Gk. text of Eph. 1:7 but not in that of Col. 1:14.

[91] The Gk. and AV have simply "for many."

[92] Since charges of Biblical "literalism" are frequently delivered against such orthodox theologians as Chytraeus, it is worthwhile to note a typical

Eph. 5:2: "Christ hath given Himself for us an offering and a sacrifice to God for a sweet-smelling savor." *These pronouncements should be kept before our eyes as a profound interpretative commentary on all the Mosaic sacrifices whenever we read Leviticus, so that we may have no doubt that each and every sacrifice was a sermon on the sacrifice and benefits of Christ.*

[4] Thus the Levitical sacrifices were also sacraments for the pious, that is, they were symbols of belief in Christ, or signs and testimonies to awaken and encourage faith in God's promised forgiveness of sins, freely given because of Christ's future death on their behalf. One thinks of Samuel who, in great distress and imminent danger from his enemies, offered a lamb as a whole burnt offering to the Lord that he might confirm his own faith and that of his people;[93] in doing this, he started them thinking about the promise of God's grace and protection and about all the benefits pledged because of Christ, the Lamb of God who takes away the sins of the world. In this regard Augustine says: "The visible sacrifice was a sacrament or sacred sign of an invisible sacrifice."[94] [5] Likewise the Levitical sacrifices were types of spiritual sacrifices and worship, i. e., of all the good works and virtues which the Holy Spirit stirs up in the saints and which are done in order to honor God. 1 Peter 2:5: "Ye are an holy priesthood, to offer up spiritual sacrifices" (not animals), "acceptable to God by Jesus Christ." Also Heb. 13:15: "Through Him we are offering[95] the sacrifice of praise to God continually"; and Hosea 14:2: "[We will render] as

example of his freedom of Scripture quotation. At the very end of section II. A. above, he renders Heb. 10:14 thus: "Unica enim oblatione perfectos efficit in perpetuum eos, qui sanctificantur"; here he renders it "Una oblatione in perpetuum consummavit sanctificatos." Such examples show that our author did not allow himself to become bound to a single rigid version of the Biblical text.

[93] 1 Sam. 7:7-12.

[94] This quotation is from Augustine's *City of God,* x. 5: "It is true that, in former times, our fathers offered up animals as victims. However, today, we Christians who read about such sacrifices but do not imitate them understand them simply as symbols of the efforts we make to attain union with God and to assist our neighbor to the same end. A visible sacrifice, therefore, is a sacrament or sacred sign of an invisible sacrifice" (op. cit., p. 123; Migne, op. cit., col. 282; cf. *City of God,* x. 19, 20).

[95] The Gk. and AV have "let us offer."

bullocks the offering of our lips confessing His name." [96] Such
sacrifices include the hearing, learning, and teaching of the true
doctrine concerning God; believing the Gospel; praying to God;
thanking Him; patiently obeying Him in the difficulties which have
to be borne — in short, consecrating our minds, wills, hearts, am-
bitions, plans, actions, and our entire lives to God, that is to say,
presenting them obedient and conformable [97] to God's word and
will. As Rom. 12:1 enjoins: "Present your bodies" (not the bodies
of dead animals, but your very selves — your souls and bodies)
"a living sacrifice, holy, acceptable unto God, which is your reasonable service." And among the other good works or services of
Love [98] which are done for our neighbor, Paul in Phil. 4:18 deems
alms [99] or acts of kindness toward believers as particularly worthy
of the name sacrifice: "I have received the gifts which were sent
from you, an odor of a sweet smell, a sacrifice [100] acceptable, well-
pleasing to God."

[6] The sacrificial system was a sign of the true church of
God, since it set the Jewish people apart from all the unbelieving
nations of the world, and since in Israel alone the true doctrine of
God and of the sacrifice and benefits of Christ was proclaimed.
The sacrifices were also [7] acts of confession (whereby the pious
declared their belief that there was only one true God who had
handed down the sure promise of redemption in Christ and the
laws of sacrifice), and [8] daily exercises in thankfulness for all
the benefits received from God. [9] But for unbelievers and the
unregenerate, the sacrifices served a tutorial function; for by
engaging in them they remained citizens of the Mosaic church and
state and were not excluded from its sacred community or civil life.
Finally [10] these sacrifices (the flesh of animals, fruit, meal, bread,
wine, olive oil, and the other things offered to God daily) were

96 The Heb. and LXX do not have "confessing His name." LXX and Syriac
read "fruit" for "bullocks." Note that this verse is 14:3 in the numeration
of the Heb. Bible and LXX.

97 Lat., *conformis* (SGLL 71).

98 Lat., *Dilectio,* "[Christian] love," used from the beginning of the fourth
century as an equivalent of ἀγάπη (SGLL 104).

99 Lat. *ele(e)mosyna* (from the Gk. ἐλεημοσύνη); see SGLL 119 and
B-J 148.

100 The word "sacrifice" has been (inadvertently?) dropped out in the text.

needed to support the Levites and other priests, who, unlike the rest of the Israelites, had not been assigned farms and fields when the promised land was apportioned; the sacrifices were therefore instrumental in maintaining a public ministry, as is amply shown in Num. 18:8-32; Deut. 18:1-8; 1 Cor. 9:11-14, and elsewhere.

The *cognates,* or analogs, of the Levitical sacrifices are to a large extent the heathen sacrifices which, by their similar rites, are seen to have spread to the gentiles from the church of the fathers.[101] For the pagans did retain sacrificial rites and ceremonies and some innate knowledge of the Law concerning right conduct in external matters,[102] even though they had lost the church's unique doctrine — namely, the promise that Christ, the woman's Seed,[103] would by His passion, death, and the sacrifice of His body placate God's wrath and that the remission of sins, reconciliation with God, liberation from sin and death, and eternal life would be freely bestowed through the Son, our Redeemer Jesus Christ, who would suffer for us.

I therefore strongly advise students to reflect now on the Homeric lines in which the poet describes the sacrificial ceremonies employed in that far-off time — ceremonies entirely consistent with the Levitical sacrifices (*Iliad,* Bks. I and II; *Odyssey,* Bk. III).[104] Herodotus (Bk. II) surveys the Egyptian sacrificial rites, and what he says concerning the heads of the victims is especially worth remembering: "Having invoked many curses on the severed head, they throw it into the river. The imprecation which they utter over the heads is, that whatever ill threatens themselves, who

---

101 Here, as often, Chytraeus uses "church" for the Jewish revelatory community in OT times; Scriptural precedent for such a usage is provided by Acts 7:38 (Schmiedel's conjectural emendation of this verse is entirely without warrant). Note that in his above statement our author does not admit the possibility of a cultic transmission in the opposite direction, with subsequent hallowing of pagan rites by revelation; or of the independent appearance of similar rites because of universal human needs. Undoubtedly Chytraeus should have given consideration to these other possibilities; but the present-day Biblical theology movement has come to see more and more evidences of the distinctiveness of the Biblical religion (cf. G. Ernest Wright's *The Old Testament Against Its Environment* [London: SCM Press, 1950]).

102 Cf. Rom. 2:14, 15.

103 In reference to the "protevangelium," Gen. 3:15.

104 The particular lines will shortly be quoted.

sacrifice, or the whole of Egypt, may fall upon that head; and from this ordinance no Egyptian will taste of the head of anything that had life." [105] This rite evidently derived from Lev. 16:20-22, where the priest, when he has placed his hand on a goat's head, confesses all the sins of the Children of Israel and calls them down on the head of the victim, etc. In general, the Israelites were accustomed to place their hands on the heads of all their sacrificial animals; and it is understandable that they also totally abstained from eating their heads and brains.

These are the above-mentioned lines from Homer:

Then, when they had prayed and had sprinkled the barley grains, they first drew back the victims' heads and cut their throats, and flayed them; and they cut out the thigh-pieces

[105] This material appears in Herodotus' *History*, ii. 39. Chytraeus gives the Greek text and a Latin translation; I have followed Godley in the English translation above. The whole of ii. 39 reads as follows: "Having brought the marked beast to the altar where the sacrifice is to be, they kindle a fire; then they pour wine on the altar over the victim and call upon the god; then they cut its throat, and having done so they sever the head from the body. They flay the carcase of the victim, then invoke many curses on its head and carry the same away. Where there is a market, and Greek traders in the place, the head is taken to the market and sold; where there are no Greeks, it is thrown into the river. The imprecation which they utter . . . may fall upon that head. In respect of the heads of sacrificed beasts and the libation of wine, the practice of all Egyptians is the same in all sacrifices; and from this ordinance no Egyptian will taste of the head of anything that had life" (*Herodotus*, with an English tr. by A. D. Godley, I [Cambridge: Harvard University Press (Loeb Classical Library), 1946], 320—323). Chytraeus' view that this Egyptian rite parallels the sacrifice described in Lev. 16:20-22, and in fact derives from it, receives confirmation in one of the foremost modern commentaries on Herodotus' *History:* "The usage of transferring 'curses' to the head of a sacrificial beast may be illustrated from the Jewish scapegoat (Lev. xvi. 21). . . . H. is wrong in supposing it to be part of all Egyptian sacrifices, for in early times the head and the haunch were especially chosen to be placed on the tables of offerings. Hence Erman . . . thinks the curse was an innovation, due to foreign (i. e., Semitic) influence" (W. W. How and J. Wells, *A Commentary on Herodotus*, corrected ed., I [Oxford: Clarendon Press, 1928], 185). How and Wells qualify Herodotus' remarks thus: "The Egyptians had no altars in the Greek sense. . . . H. is wrong in making the refusal to eat the head universal; but it was sometimes given away . . . and it certainly appears less often than the other joints" (ibid.). For a general statement on the reliability of Bk. II of Herodotus' *History*, see Wilhelm Spiegelberg, *The Credibility of Herodotus' Account of Egypt*, trans. with additions by A. M. Blackman (Oxford: Blackwell, 1927).

and covered them with a double layer of fat, and laid raw flesh thereon. These they burned on billets of wood stripped of leaves, and the inner parts they pierced with spits, and held them over the flame of Hephaestus. But when the thigh-pieces were wholly burned and they had tasted of the inner parts, they cut up the rest and spitted it, and roasted it carefully, and drew all off the spits. Then, when they had ceased from their labour and had made ready the meal, they feasted, nor did their hearts lack aught of the equal feast. But when they had put from them the desire of food and drink, the youths filled the bowls brim full of drink and served out to all, first pouring drops for libation into the cups. So the whole day long they sought to appease the god with song, singing the beautiful paean, the sons of the Achaeans.[106]

C. *Mistaken Ideas About Sacrifice*

Among opposing viewpoints we have, first, the Epicurean and Cyclopean contempt toward God and toward sacrifices commanded by God; as Euripides' Cyclops says:

> And as for Zeus's thunder — I've no fear
> Of that, sir stranger! it's by no means clear
> To me that he's a mightier god than I.
> I sacrifice beasts to my great Self,
> And to no god beside — except, that is,
> My belly, greatest of all deities.[107]

[106] These Homeric lines (sixteen are quoted) constitute *Iliad,* i. 458—461, 464—473; *Iliad,* ii. 421—432; and *Odyssey,* iii. 447, 457 b, 458, 461, 462, 473. Chytraeus gives the Greek text without translation; I have followed the translation given in *Homer: The Iliad,* with an English tr. by A. T. Murray, I (London: Heinemann; Cambridge, Mass.: Harvard University Press [Loeb Classical Library], 1924), 36—39, 82, 83; cf. *Homer: The Odyssey,* with an English tr. by A. T. Murray, I (London, Heinemann; New York, Putnam [Loeb Classical Library], 1924), 100—103. Murray's text differs in a few particulars from that of Chytraeus, but the variants are minor and do not affect the sense of the passage.

[107] Chytraeus here quotes in Greek and gives in Latin translation lines 320, 321 and 334, 335 of Euripides' *Cyclops,* the single surviving example of the Greek Satyric Drama. The English translation above is substantially that of A. S. Way: *Euripides,* with an English tr. by Arthur S. Way, II (Cambridge, Harvard University Press [Loeb Classical Library], 1912),

Then there are all the superstitious and idolatrous opinions on sacrifice which attribute to sacrificial rites themselves the power to merit remission of sins, placate God's wrath, and render Him propitious, and which associate with this error other impious beliefs. Since these views have spread widely and continue to do so in every age, not only among the heathen majority of mankind but

550—553. The Cyclops' entire speech (ll. 316—346) is a classic statement of hedonistic egocentrism:

> Wealth, master Shrimp, is to the truly wise
> The one true god; the rest are mockeries
> Of tall talk, naught but mere word-pageantries.
> As for my father's fanes by various seas,
> *That* for them! — why d'ye talk to me of these?
> And as for Zeus's thunder — I've no fear
> Of that, sir stranger! it's by no means clear
> To me that he's a mightier god than I;
> So I don't care for him; I'll tell you why: —
> When he pours down his rain from yonder sky,
> I have snug lodgings in this cave of mine.
> On roasted veal or some wild game I dine,
> Then drench my belly, sprawling on my back,
> With a whole butt of milk. His thunder-crack —
> I answer it, when he splits the clouds asunder,
> With boomings of my cavern-shaking thunder.
> And when the north-east wind pours down the snow,
> I wrap my body round with furs, and so
> I light my fire, and naught for snow I care.
> And, willy-nilly, earth has got to bear
> The grass that makes my sheep and cattle fat.
> I sacrifice to my great Self, sir Sprat,
> And to no god beside — except, that is,
> My belly, greatest of all deities.
> Eat plenty and drink plenty every day,
> And never worry — *that* is, so I say,
> The Zeus that suits a level-headed man;
> But as for those who framed an artful plan
> Of laws, to puzzle plain men's lives with these —
> I snap my thumb at them. I'll never cease
> Seeking my own soul's good — by eating you.
> And, as for guest-gifts, you shall have your due —
> Oh no, I won't be niggard! — a hot fire,
> And yonder caldron, which my Sea-god sire
> Will fill up with his special private brew
> To make your chop-steaks into a savoury stew.
> Now, toddle in, and all stand ready near
> The Paunch-god's altar, and make your host good cheer.

even in the body of the church, it is essential that we recognize and clearly refute them. In order, therefore, to achieve greater lucidity in this presentation, I shall distinguish six principal errors with regard to sacrifices and to ceremonies in general — errors which are commonly and extensively embraced by the heathen, and, in the church, by Judaizers, Pharisees, monks, and every kind of hypocrite, whether layman or cleric.

(1) The first erroneous idea has to do with the efficient cause of sacrifice.[108] It is that men may, of their own free will and honest effort (as they say), choose [t] and establish their own divine worship and sacrifices not commanded by God's express word — as the Israelites from time to time carried out new religious rites and sacrifices in Bethel, Gilgal, and Beer-sheba, and as they chose the Baal cult and others in order to engage in many pious exercises and more zealously and ardently to worship the true God by that variety of activities. This viewpoint the prophets criticize with utmost severity; they teach that God wants to be acknowledged, prayed to, and worshiped only in the manner which He has taught in His own Word and that all sacrifices and religious worship contrived by men apart from God's word are impious and idolatrous.[109] Deut.[u] 12:32: "What thing I command you, observe to do it only unto the Lord; thou shalt not add thereto nor diminish from it." Also Ezek. 20:19, 18: "Walk in My statutes. Walk ye not in the statutes of your fathers, neither observe their judgments"; Is. 29:13, 14: "Forasmuch as they have worshiped Me with the doctrines and precepts of men, therefore the wisdom of their wise men shall perish"; Matt. 15:9: "In vain they do worship Me with the commandments of men"; Titus 1:14: "Ye shall not give heed to commandments of men that turn from the truth."

(2) The second error involves the formal cause [110] and may be stated thus: Sacrifices and ceremonies, whether commanded by God or contrived and chosen by men apart from God's Word, are

[108] See above, note 70.

[109] It has been well said that the popular notion that the various religions are "like many roads leading to the same place" is true only if the place is hell and we exclude the Christian faith; our author's belief that a qualitative distinction exists between Christian and non-Christian religion is fully supported by John 14:6 and Acts 4:12. Cf. note 79 above.

[110] See above, note 82 and the text corresponding.

per se God-pleasing works and God-honoring worship — that they are such *ex opere operato* (as they say), i. e., even if true repentance, true faith, and moral obedience are not present in the heart of the worshiper.[111] This crass error — which, nonetheless, was very widely spread even among the Jewish people — is clearly refuted not only by the divine Word but also by the statements of all sensible pagans. Prov. 15:8: "The sacrifices of the wicked are abominations before God." It follows that sacrifices or other external acts in themselves do not please God at all unless one already has a believing heart, is reconciled to God by faith, and is morally obedient in the inner man. Gen. 4:7: "If thou art good, thy sacrifice shall be accepted; but if thou art evil. . . ."[112] Is. 1:11, 13, 15: "To what purpose is the multitude of your sacrifices unto Me? Incense is an abomination unto Me; for your hands are full of blood. . . ." Jer. 7:9-11, 21-23: "Ye are wont to steal, murder, and commit adultery, and swear falsely, and sacrifice unto Baal, and walk after other gods; and ye come and stand before Me in this house of worship and say, We are delivered though we have done [113] all these abominations.[114] Is then this house become a den of robbers? . . . Thus saith the Lord: I commanded not your fathers in the day that I brought them out of the land of Egypt concerning burnt offerings or sacrifices" (i. e., that they were to be offered with the idea that they constitute divine worship in themselves and merit the remission of sins and placate God's wrath *ex opere operato* — even when those who offer them lack true repentance and give free rein to all their iniquities). "But this commanded I them, saying, Obey My voice, and I will be your God, and ye shall be My people; and walk ye in all the ways that I have commanded you that it may be well unto you."

In addition, similar statements can be cited from the pagan

111 See below, note 240.

112 Chytraeus' rendering of this verse is more in the nature of an interpretation of it; the Heb. reads: "If thou doest well, shalt thou not be accepted? And if thou doest not well," etc. (the Hiphil of יטב appears in the protasis of both conditions).

113 The AV, following the Heb., has: "We are delivered to do [עֲשׂוֹת לְמַעַן] all these abominations."

114 The AV, following the Heb., punctuates this sentence as a question ("Will ye steal . . . ?").

world. Though these contain only Law and do not present the unique wisdom of the Gospel concerning the knowledge of Christ and concerning faith, it is good for us to examine them; for by doing so we may perceive that the false ᵛ sacrificial ideas just mentioned are refuted even by the judgment of human reason.

Aristotle says in his *Rhetorica:* οὐκ εἰκὸς τὸν θεὸν χαίρειν ταῖς δαπάναις τῶν θυομένων, ἀλλὰ ταῖς εὐσεβείαις τῶν θυόντων ("It is reasonable to suppose that God rejoices, not in the costliness of the sacrifices but in the piety of those who offer them").[115]

Plato writes in his *Alcibiades:* οὐ παράγεται ὁ θεὸς ὑπὸ δώρων, ὡς τοκιστής, ἀλλ' ἀποβλέπει πρὸς τὴν ψυχήν, ἄν τις ὅσιος καὶ δίκαιος ὢν τυγχάνῃ ("God is not won over or diverted by gifts, like some usurer, but regards the soul, whether a man is just and pure"). And in the same passage he says that the εὐφημία [silent worship], that is, prayers and thanksgiving, of

115 Here Chytraeus quotes not Aristotle's *Art of Rhetoric (Rhetorica),* but the *De Rhetorica ad Alexandrum* (1423 b. 25), a work which, though still attributed by some modern scholars to Aristotle (e. g., Thomas Case in the *Encyclopaedia Britannica,* 11th ed.), is today generally considered the work of some other author. "We shall probably not be far wrong if, accepting a date slightly anterior to 300 B.C., we attribute the work to a Peripatetic writer contemporaneous with Theophrastus. The treatise has certainly many points of contact with the *Rhetorica* and assumes and supplements Aristotle's classification; it is written from a more practical and less philosophic standpoint and in the spirit of Socrates rather than of Aristotle" (E. S. Forster, in the Preface to his translation of the *De Rhetorica ad Alexandrum,* in *The Works of Aristotle,* ed. W. D. Ross, Vol. XI [Oxford: Clarendon Press, 1924]). In quoting and translating the Greek text, Chytraeus changes "gods" to "God." One should note that the author of *De Rhetorica ad Alexandrum* gives the quoted statement as one argument which can be used "when we are urging a reduction of the scale of our sacred rites"; but he also gives arguments for "maintaining that the existing form should be retained" and for "advising a change to greater magnificence in the celebration of sacred rites." He goes on to define the ideal sacrifice thus: "The best sacrifice of all is one which is pious towards the gods, moderate in costliness, likely to bring advantage in war, and splendid from a spectacular point of view. It will be pious towards the gods, if ancestral usage is not violated; it will be moderate in costliness, if the accompaniments of the ceremony are not all wasted; it will be splendid from a spectacular point of view, if gold and such things as are not actually consumed are used lavishly; and it will be advantageous for war, if horsemen and infantry in full panoply accompany the procession."

the Lacedaemonians please God better than the ever-so-costly sacrifices of the Athenians.[116]

[116] This material is included in the *Alcibiades II*, 149, 150. Jowett writes: "That the Dialogue which goes by the name of the Second Alcibiades is a genuine writing of Plato will not be maintained by any modern critic"; however, it is to be included among "examples of Platonic dialogues to be assigned probably to the second or third generation after Plato, when his writings were well known at Athens and Alexandria" and is especially interesting because it "shows that the difficulties about prayer which have perplexed Christian theologians were not unknown among the followers of Plato" (op. cit., p. 791). The passage from which Chytraeus quotes above is worth reproducing here *in extenso* (Knight's translation, ibid., pp. 803, 804):

> And now I will relate to you a story which I have heard from certain of our elders. It chanced that when the Athenians and Lacedaemonians were at war, our city lost every battle by land and sea and never gained a victory. The Athenians being annoyed and perplexed how to find a remedy for their troubles, decided to send and enquire at the shrine of Ammon. Their envoys were also to ask, "Why the Gods always granted the victory to the Lacedaemonians?" "We," (they were to say,) "offer them more and finer sacrifices than any other Hellenic state, and adorn their temples with gift·, as nobody else does; moreover, we make the most solemn and costly processions to them every year, and spend more money in their service than all the rest of the Hellenes put together. But the Lacedaemonians take no thought of such matters, and pay so little respect to the Gods that they have a habit of sacrificing blemished animals to them, and in various ways are less zealous than we are, although their wealth is quite equal to ours." When they had thus spoken, and had made their request to know what remedy they could find against the evils which troubled them, the prophet made no direct answer, — clearly because he was not allowed by the God to do so; — but he summoned them to him and said: "Thus saith Ammon to the Athenians: 'The silent worship of the Lacedaemonians pleaseth me better than all the offerings of the other Hellenes.'" Such were the words of the God, and nothing more. He seems to have meant by "silent worship" the prayer of the Lacedaemonians, which is indeed widely different from the usual requests of the Hellenes. For they either bring to the altar bulls with gilded horns or make offerings to the Gods, and beg at random for what they need, good or bad. When, therefore, the Gods hear them using words of ill omen they reject these costly processions and sacrifices of theirs. And we ought, I think, to be very careful

The following noble assertion is taken from Zaleucus, the Locrian legislator: οὐ θεραπεύεται ὁ θεὸς δαπάναις κ.τ.λ. ἀλλὰ ἀρετῇ καὶ προαιρέσει τῶν καλῶν ἔργων καὶ δικαίων. διὸ ἕκαστον δεῖ ἀγαθὸν εἶναι καὶ πράξει καὶ προαιρέσει τὸν μέλλοντα ἔσεσθαι θεοφιλῆ.[117]

In Letter 95, Seneca writes: "The first act of worship to God is to believe in Him: the next to present to Him the counterpart of His greatness and of the goodness without which there is no greatness. Would you win God to your side? Be good. He worships Him enough who makes Him his pattern." [118]

> and consider well what we should say and what leave unsaid. Homer, too, will furnish us with similar stories. For he tells us how the Trojans in making their encampment,
>
>> Offered up whole hecatombs to the immortals, and how the "sweet savour" was borne "to the heavens by the winds";
>
>> But the blessed Gods were averse and received it not. For exceedingly did they hate the holy Ilium, Both Priam and the people of the spear-skilled king.
>
> So that it was in vain for them to sacrifice and offer gifts, seeing that they were hateful to the Gods, who are not, like vile usurers, to be gained over by bribes. And it is foolish for us to boast that we are superior to the Lacedaemonians by reason of our much worship. The idea is inconceivable that the Gods have regard, not to the justice and purity of our souls, but to costly processions and sacrifices, which men may celebrate year after year, although they have committed innumerable crimes against the Gods or against their fellowmen or the state.

[117] Chytraeus gives this passage without Latin translation. It may be rendered as follows: "God is not conciliated by extravagance, etc., but by virtue and the deliberate choice of good and righteous actions. For this reason each person who would be dear to God must be good both in practice and in intention" (my translation). The name Zaleucus is misprinted "Zaleuius" in the text. He was a "lawgiver of Italian Locri. As his laws are said to have been the first Greek eodification, he probably lived ca. 650 B.C." (OCD 964). His statement quoted above comes down to us in the *Anthology* of Stobaeus, which was probably composed in the 5th century A.D. For the quotation see *Ioannis Stobaei Anthologii libri duo posteriores*, recensuit Otto Hense, II [Vol. IV of the Stobaeus edition by Wachsmuth and Hense] (Berlin: Weidmann, 1909), p. 124, ll. 8—13.

[118] These remarks appear in Seneca's *Epistolae ad Lucilium*, xcv. 50. Chytraeus cites the letter as number 96; this has been changed to 95 in the text above. The translation I have given follows that of Barker: *Seneca's Letters to Lucilius*, trans. E. Phillips Barker, II (Oxford: Clarendon Press,

(3) The third error with regard to sacrifice concerns its final cause [119] or results. Proponents of this error argue that sacrifices, the slaying of animals, masses, and so on, merit the remission of sins, placate God's wrath, render Him propitious, and are recompenses and compensations for sins committed. This loathsome, insane opinion is condemned by the entire Gospel, which teaches that the sacrifice of our Lord Jesus Christ, the one and only Son [120] of God, offered once for all for us on the altar of the cross, has placated God's wrath and earned the remission of sins and eternal salvation for the church. Heb. 10:4, 14: "It is not possible that the blood of bulls and of goats should take away sin," but Christ "by one offering hath perfected" (that is, hath completely justified and saved) "forever them that are sanctified." Also Heb. 9:26: "Once in the end of the world hath Christ appeared to put away sin by the sacrifice of Himself"; Is. 66:3: "He that killeth an ox" (that is, with the idea that he earns the remission of sins by that sacrifice) "is as if he slew a man"; Rom. 3:24, 25: "We are being justified freely by God's grace through the redemption accomplished by Christ Jesus, whom God hath set forth to be a propitiation through faith in His blood"; Rom. 8:3: [121] "God sent His own Son in the likeness of sinful flesh, and for this sin offering" [122] (i. e., because of His Son, who was the sacrifice for sin) "condemned and destroyed [123] sin in the flesh . . ."; Ps. 40:6-8 and Heb. 10:5 ff.: [124] "Sacrifice and offering Thou didst not desire; Mine ears

1932), 155; it should be noted that as usual Chytraeus changes the pagan "gods" to "God" in his quotation. Lucius Annaeus Seneca (ca. 3 B. C. to A. D. 65), it will be remembered, was a Stoic philosopher and Roman statesman, many of whose ethical statements are so lofty that some of the early church fathers believed him to have been a Christian — with the result that a forged correspondence between St. Paul and Seneca was produced.

[119] I. e., end/purpose.

[120] The text misprints *Filius* for *Filii* here.

[121] See above, Section II. A. 2.

[122] In the Gk. this phrase is better taken with the preceding clause: "God sent His own Son in the likeness of sinful flesh and for sin/for a sin offering, and condemned sin in the flesh."

[123] Our author's *damnavit & abolevit* well renders the Gk. κατέκρινεν in Rom. 8:3; see A-G 413, where "pronounced His judgment on" is employed in the translation of this verse.

[124] See above, note 64.

hast Thou opened; burnt offering and sin offering hast Thou not required. Then said I, Lo, I come. In the volume of the book it is written of Me, that I should do Thy will. I have delighted to do it, O My God.[125] By this will we are sanctified through the offering of the body of Jesus Christ once for all."

(4) The fourth error is that sacrifices and ceremonies (whether the product of God's command or man's picking and choosing) are better and more God-pleasing works than are the obligations of love toward one's neighbor and the responsibilities of family and state. Against this very common belief let us consider Scriptural evidences which prove that *good works — works of divine love and kindness toward one's neighbor — as well as activities required in every divinely established vocation, are, when performed with the fear of God and faith in Him truly illuminating them, far greater and more excellent means of worshiping God than all the sacrifices and other works of all the monks rolled into one — indeed, they surpass even the sacrificial rites instituted by the divine Word.* (Examples of God-honoring vocational activities are the efforts of teachers to impart and spread God's doctrine and other arts essential for living; the tasks of pious magistrates who govern, judge, and punish; the work of mothers in bringing up their children and running their households; the labors of farmers, and of menservants and maidservants who perform domestic functions; etc.)[126] Prov. 21:3: "To do mercy[127] and judgment is more acceptable to the Lord than sacrifices." Hos. 6:6: "I desire mercy and not sacrifice; and the knowledge of God more than burnt offerings" (the verse is quoted by Christ in Matt. 12:7; 9:13, and elsewhere[128] when He refutes this very error on the part of the Pharisees)." Ps. 50:8, 13-15: "I will not reprove thee for thy sacrifices. . . . Will I eat the flesh of bulls or drink the blood of goats? Offer unto God thanksgiving, and pay thy vows unto the Most High.

---

125 The Vulgate of Ps. 40:7, 8 is here followed.

126 See note 268.

127 Heb. צְדָקָה — "righteousness" (AV: "justice"). The element of mercy is not absent from the concept, however, as Paul Ramsey has shown (*Basic Christian Ethics* [New York: Scribner, 1950], pp. 2—24, especially p. 9).

128 Matt. 9:13 and 12:7 are the only direct uses of Hos. 6:6 in the NT; perhaps Chytraeus is thinking of passages such as Matt. 23:23 which express the same idea but in fact rely on other OT sources (e. g., Micah 6:6-8).

Call upon Me in the day of trouble. . . ." Is. 1:11, 16, 17: "To what purpose is the multitude of your sacrifices unto Me? Wash you, make you clean; put away the evil of your thinking [129] from before Mine eyes; cease to do evil; begin [130] to do well; seek judgment, relieve the oppressed. . . ." In Matt. 15:1-9 Christ reproaches the Pharisees, who were teaching that it was more virtuous to present something to the temple than to support one's needy parents.

(5) The fifth mistaken idea is that sacrifices and other ceremonial observances are acts of righteousness [131] before God — or that the Mosaic rites are essential to the righteousness of the Gospel and to salvation. This error is condemned by the clear decree of the apostolic council (Acts 15:11): "We believe that through the grace of our Lord Jesus Christ we are saved, even as the fathers were saved." [132] Paul says the same throughout his Epistle to the Galatians: "We know that a man is not justified by the works of the Law but by the faith of Jesus Christ"; "Behold, I, Paul, say unto you, that if ye be circumcised, Christ shall profit you nothing"; "For in Christ neither circumcision availeth anything, nor uncircumcision, but faith which worketh by love." [133]

{The Abrogation of the Levitical Sacrifices} [x]

God abolished the entire Mosaic polity, together with its sacrifices and forensic laws, [134] for this very reason — so that they

---

[129] Heb. מַעַלְלֵיכֶם — "of your doings."

[130] Heb. לִמְדוּ — "learn."

[131] The plural *iusticiae* would seem preferable here (cf. SGLL 223).

[132] The Gk. says simply "even as they"; Chytraeus takes the "they" to refer to "the fathers" (as do St. Augustine and Calvin), but modern interpretations tend to make the Gentile Christians the referent of the pronoun. See EG II, 320.

[133] Gal. 2:16; 5:2, 6.

[134] The orthodox Lutheran dogmatician David Hollaz (1646—1713) writes: "The *Forensic* or *Judicial Law* is the command of God, by which He bound the Israelites in the times of the Old Testament, and through Moses prescribed to them a form of political government, so that external discipline might be preserved in civil society, and that the Jewish polity, in which Christ was to be born, might be distinguished from the polity of other nations. The forensic Law uttered precepts concerning all those things which pertained to the administration of the Israelitic republic, and came

would not be thought necessary for one's salvation and righteousness before God. Dan. 9:27: "Messiah shall cause the sacrifice and the oblation to cease, and the city shall be desolated." [135] Jer. 31: 31, 32: "Behold, the days will come, saith the Lord, that I will make a new covenant with the house of Israel and with the house of Judah, not according to the covenant that I made with your [136] fathers when I brought them out of Egypt. . . ." The Epistle to the Hebrews interprets this passage as follows: "In that He saith, A new covenant, He hath made the first old. Now that which decayeth and waxeth old is ready to vanish away." [137] Heb. 7:11, 12, 18, 19: "If perfection" (true righteousness and eternal salvation) "were by the Levitical priesthood (for under it the Law was commended [138] to the people), what further need was there that another priest should rise after the order of Melchisedec and not be called after the order of Aaron? Verily, the priesthood being changed, there is made of necessity a change also of the Law; and there is a disannulling of the commandment going before for the weakness and unprofitableness thereof. For the Law made nothing perfect." The sacrifices of the Law brought no one true and perfect righteousness or freedom from sin; but they were shadows of the Christ,[139] "by whom we come unto God." [140]

(6) Today many argue that the propitiatory sacrifice of Christ is applied to others in every age through the ceremonial rites of priests — that the Levitical sacrifices, therefore, though not

under the cognizance of the forum or court of the Jews." (Quoted in Heinrich Schmid, *The Doctrinal Theology of the Evangelical Lutheran Church*, trans. Hay and Jacobs, 5th ed. [Philadelphia: United Lutheran Publication House, 1899], p. 512)

[135] The last clause, which is difficult in the Heb., probably refers to the desolation of the temple rather than that of the city (cf. Edward J. Young's remarks in Francis Davidson's *The New Bible Commentary* [Grand Rapids: Eerdmans, 1953], p. 679); but in any case Dan. 9:26 asserts that both the sanctuary and the city shall be destroyed.

[136] Heb. and AV: "their."

[137] Heb. 8:13. The Jeremiah quotation comprises Heb. 8:8-12.

[138] The 4th (supine) principal part of *sancio* is here given as *sancitum* rather than the CL. *sanctum*. See note 71 above.

[139] Cf. Heb. 8:4, 5; 10:1; Col. 2:16, 17.

[140] Heb. 7:25; cf. 7:19.

meritorious in the remission of sins, were the means of applying such remission. This argument Christ Himself plainly judges in John 17:19, 20, where He makes application of His own sacrifice in the prayer: "For their sakes I sanctify Myself that they also might be sanctified. Neither pray I for these alone but for all them which shall believe on Me through their word." Also note Rom. 3:25: "God hath set forth Christ to be a propitiation through faith in His blood." Thus the Old Testament fathers applied the benefits of Christ to themselves by their personal faith, and the sacrificial rites were not applicatory means in themselves. (This matter is treated more fully below in our discussion of the sacrifice of the Mass.) And at this point we conclude our examination of the Levitical sacrificial system.

III

THE PRIESTHOOD AND SACRIFICE
OF CHRIST

A. *Definitions and Distinctions*

Priesthood in the general sense refers to the divinely established office of teaching the doctrine which God has handed down, i. e., the Law and the Gospel of Christ;[y] of praying to God for oneself and others (the promise being that one will certainly be heard); and of offering particular sacrifices commanded by God (thereby declaring that the One whom the priest so worships is truly God). Now these are the three principal duties of priests,[141] and they are duties common to all Christians or believers, whether living before or after the birth of Christ. These all are equally priests, in respect to their right of teaching and confessing the Gospel, praying for themselves and others, and presenting thank offerings to God; this we shall show at greater length a little later when we deal with the universal priesthood of all Christians.

Although this description of priesthood applies to all Christians equally, because Christ, the only true High Priest, has conferred the honor and right of priesthood upon them, we must add to the foregoing definition certain individualizing elements which distinguish Christ as Priest from Aaron and other believers. Therefore we present the following: *The High Priest of the church is the only-begotten Son of God, our Lord Jesus Christ, who was ordained directly by the eternal Father (Heb. 5:4-9), and anointed with the fullness of the Holy Spirit (John 3:34; Col. 2:9,3), that He might {i} reveal to the human race the mystery of God's will concerning the redemption and salvation of men and teach the*

---

[141] This point has been made above, section I. C. With the reference, here and in that section, to Law and Gospel as both contained in the Old Testament, as well as both in the New, see Luther's "Sermon on the Distinction between the Law and the Gospel"; and C. F .W. Walther's classic, *The Proper Distinction between Law and Gospel,* ed. W. H. T. Dau (St. Louis: Concordia, 1928).

Gospel brought forth by Him from the bosom of the Father (John 6:38-40; John 1:18 [142]); {ii} on entering the Holy of Holies (Heb. 9:11, 12, 24) intercede and pray for the whole church (Heb. 7: 24, 25) — the promise being that He is certainly heard (John 11:42); {iii} once for all offer the only sacrifice, namely Himself, by which He might placate God's wrath against the sins of men and earn the remission of sins, righteousness, and eternal life for the whole church (Heb. 9:12; 7:27; 10:11, 12, 14); and {iv} apply these benefits of His to believers (John 17:19, 20), kindle true knowledge and love of God in the hearts of those who embrace the Gospel (Matt. 11:27), and regard the prayers of those who call upon Him (John 14:13). The Scriptural testimonies, by which the elements of this definition are linked together, clearly show the difference between the high priesthood of Aaron and that of Christ, and the several units of the definition, with their corresponding references, distinguish Christ from Aaron and all other priests.

In the Epistle to the Hebrews the entire doctrine of Christ's priesthood and a comparison of it with the Aaronic or Levitical priesthood are set forth at length; from this source I have extracted the following points of difference. [1][r] First, with regard to dignity of person, Christ the High Priest surpasses to the greatest degree Aaron and the Levitical priests. For Christ is not just a weak and mortal man as they were, but in fact the only-begotten Son of God, truly and by nature God, Creator and Preserver of all things, and more excellent than all angels and men — even Levites. Christ had Melchizedek as a type — Melchizedek who blesses Abraham and as the patriarch's superior accepts tithes from him and thereby from the Levites also (see Heb. 1:1—2:10; 7:1-28). "The Law hath made men priests which have infirmity; but the word of the oath hath made the Son, who is perfected forevermore" (Heb. 7:28; God's oath occurs in Ps. 110:4 and Ps. 2:7). [2] Therefore Christ was ordained to His priesthood on the basis of a far more sublime call than were the Levitical priests. Specifically, He was called not through human agents but by the eternal voice of God the Father which proclaimed from heaven: "Thou art My Son; this day have

[142] The text gives this reference as John 3 instead of John 1; the error has been rectified in the translation. All of the verses designated above in parentheses are fully written out in the text; however, it has seemed unnecessary here (and in several other instances as well) to provide more than the references in our translation.

I begotten Thee. Ask of Me, and I shall give Thee the heathen for Thine inheritance" — God's oath having been added to this effect.[143] Ps. 110:4: "The Lord hath sworn and will not repent, Thou art a Priest forever after the order of Melchizedek."

[3] Then as to office, benefits, and efficacy of priesthood, Christ and the Levitical priests especially differ from each other (Heb. 8; 9; and 7). For Christ is the *grace-giving* Priest of the new covenant, who by His own intercession and sacrifice has secured for us God's favor, the remission of sins, complete liberation from sin and death, everlasting righteousness, and consummate life and salvation; and He declares and offers these benefits of His to us by the word of the Gospel which He brought forth from the bosom of the eternal Father, and imparts them to us by His own power and efficacy. But the Levitical priesthood is chiefly a ministry of the Law — manifesting and disclosing sin, and every year, by the same sacrifices, bringing back the memory of sins and the death to which we all are subject because of sin — not taking away sin and death but serving only as a σκιαγραφία [sketch][144] of the true and heavenly priesthood of Christ. Heb. 10:1-4, 11, 12, 14: "The Law, having a shadow of good things to come and not the very image of the things, can never with those sacrifices which they offer year by year continually make the comers thereunto perfect. For then would they not have ceased to be offered? But in those sacrifices there is a remembrance again made of sins every year. For it is not possible that the blood of bulls and of goats should take away sins. . . . The Levitical priests stand daily ministering and offering oftentimes the same sacrifices, which can never take away sins. But Christ, after He has offered one sacrifice for sins, forever[145] sits down on the right hand of God. For by one offering He hath perfected forever them that are being sanctified," that is, He has fully and completely justified and sanctified them — wholly freed them from sin and death and bestowed perfect righteousness and

143 Ps. 2:7, 8. Quoted at Christ's baptism (Matt. 3:17; Mark 1:11; Luke 3:22) and transfiguration (Matt. 17:5; Mark 9:7; Luke 9:35; 2 Peter 1:17).

144 Chytraeus has σκιογραφία for σκιαγραφία; this error has been corrected in the translation. A σκιαγραφία (from σκιά, "shadow") is a sketch or rough painting such as produces an effect at a distance; it is so used by Plato.

145 See above, note 69.

life upon them as the elect. Heb. 7:11, 18, 19: "If perfection were by the Levitical priesthood," i. e., if the Levitical priesthood had really been able to justify and sanctify, "what further need was there that another priest [146] should rise after the order of Melchisedec and not be called after the order of Aaron? For there is a disannulling of the commandment going before" (that is, the Levitical priesthood) "for the weakness and unprofitableness thereof. For the Law made nothing perfect," i. e., justifies and sanctifies no one truly and completely, "but there was the introduction of a better hope, by the which we draw nigh unto God."

These distinctions of office between Christ and the Levitical priests can be described and enumerated more fully. For [4] Christ is the source and prime author of the Gospel doctrine which was brought forth by Him from the bosom of the Father; other priests, receiving it from this Sun and Light of the world Himself, learn and propagate it. Then [5] Christ approaches the eternal Father without a mediator and intercedes for the human race with the knowledge that the φιλόστοργος [tenderly loving] [147] Father will refuse His dearest and only-begotten Son nothing. But other priests approach God in the wake of the Son of God, who acts as Guide and Mediator, and by trust in Christ the Mediator seek and await God's favor and other good gifts from Him. Further [6], Christ is the unique and eternal Priest who has an everlasting priesthood, "wherefore He is able also to save them to the uttermost that come unto God by Him, seeing He ever liveth to make intercession for them" (Heb. 7:25). But the Levitical priests were "many, because they were not suffered to continue by reason of death" (Heb. 7:23). Also [7], the Levitical priests sacrifice dead animals to God, and these can never take away sins; but Christ did not offer the blood of bulls and of goats but, in shedding His own blood, "through the eternal Spirit offered Himself without spot to God" (Heb. 9:13, 14). Besides [8], the Levitical priests sacrifice the same victims often — victims which can never cleanse the conscience from sins or produce true righteousness and life; Christ, however, offered Himself once only and "by the one offering hath

[146] The text has *Sacerdotum* misprinted for *Sacerdotem*.

[147] The Gk. word refers to the love of parents and children, brothers and sisters.

perfected forever them that are to be sanctified" (Heb. 10:14).[148]
Moreover [9], the Levitical priests offer up sacrifices first for their
own sins and then for the people's; but Christ, a Priest who is
"holy, harmless, undefiled, separate from sinners," offered up Himself once to God, not for His own benefit but for the sins of the
whole world (Heb. 7:26, 27). Finally [10], the Levitical priests
serve in a tabernacle made with hands which is a figure and shadow
of heavenly things; but Christ, a Priest of good and eternal things,
"by a greater and more perfect tabernacle, not of this building,[149]
entered into heaven itself, now to appear in the presence of God
for us."

To this point, I have in various ways set forth a description
of the High Priest. Now in addition I shall present instruction
concerning Christ's sacrifice: *The sacrifice of Christ is the action
whereby the High Priest of the church, Jesus Christ our Lord, the
Son of God, in transferring to Himself God's terrible wrath against
all the sins of all mankind and obeying God in the bitterest
torments* [150] *of soul and the death of the body, offers Himself to
the eternal Father on the altar of the cross; and by this offering or
act of obedience in His passion and death makes satisfaction for the
sins of men, placates God's ever so just wrath, propitiates Him,
and gains for men the remission of sins, freedom from sin and death,
justification, and life eternal.* This definition is confirmed by clear
testimonies in Hebrews 9; 10; 5; 7; and elsewhere.

B. *An Anatomy of Christ's Sacrifice*

Although in this life we cannot at all thoroughly investigate
the causes of this wonderful divine plan which necessitated the
sacrifice of God's Son, our Lord Jesus Christ, yet some of the
reasons — those which God reveals in His Word — ought to be
pondered reverently.

The *efficient principal cause* [151] of Christ's sacrifice is the will

---

[148] The Gk. has simply "are being sanctified," and Chytraeus normally so
translates it in quoting the verse.

[149] The *sed* in the text at this point must be dropped in translating; it
results from the blending of Heb. 9:11 and Heb. 9:24 which here takes place.

[150] Lat., *cruciatus,* from *crux* ("cross").

[151] *"Principal cause,* a cause which works by the power of its own form
and makes the effect in some way like itself. If it be an intelligent cause,

of God's Son, who voluntarily turned upon Himself the wrath of God against sin and underwent abuse and dreadful torments [150] of soul and body, so as to make satisfaction for the sins of the human race and, with the placation of God's wrath, restore righteousness and eternal life to men.[152] John 10:15: "I lay down My life for the sheep." Is. 53:7: "He was sacrificed because He Himself willed it." [153] Ps. 40:8: "I have delighted to do Thy will, O My God."

The *interior motivating cause* [154] which actuated the will of God's Son so that He became a Priest and Sacrifice for us is God's ardent love and limitless mercy — a love and mercy properly related to divine justice. For when mankind, because it had fallen into sin, was to have been abandoned to everlasting punishment by the immutable decree of justice, the Son of God had compassion on man and took the ever so just wrath of God and the punishments upon Himself, in order that He might satisfy God's justice and we might be spared because of Him. John 3:16: "God so loved the world that He gave His only-begotten Son." Eph. 5:2: "Christ hath loved us and hath given Himself for us an offering and a sacrifice to God." 1 John 4:9, 10: "In this is manifested the love of God toward us, not that we ourselves [155] have loved God

it also intends the effect, acts by its own initiative, and controls the instruments to its own purposes." (Wuellner, *Dictionary of Scholastic Philosophy,* p. 19.) For the meaning of "efficient cause," see above, note 70.

[152] The use of imperfect subjunctives after a present main verb in this sentence, though uncommon and a violation of strict sequence of tenses, is found on occasion even in Cicero. All-Gren suggests (p. 306) that when this occurs "the writer is thinking of past time"; that is precisely the case here, for Chytraeus' attention is centered on the once-for-all sacrificial act of Christ on the cross.

[153] Our author's Latin rendering here (it is the Vulgate text) incorrectly assumes (1) that the Heb. נִגַּשׂ ("He was oppressed") is נִגַּשׁ ("He was sacrificed" [!]), and (2) that the Heb. וַיַּעֲנֶה is from the verb עָנָה ("be responsive/amenable/docile"), whereas it is from the homonymous root meaning "be afflicted"; thus the AV correctly translates: "He was oppressed and He was afflicted." Of course, the oppression was by sacrifice, and the affliction was voluntary, as the other passages quoted by Chytraeus show.

[154] Lat., *causa impulsiva interior.* The exterior and the interior causes refer respectively to "the cause influencing a thing from the outside and the cause active within itself" (D-B 140).

but that He Himself [155] has loved us and has sent His Son to be the propitiation for our sins." Rom. 5:8: "God commendeth His love toward us in that, while we were sinners, Christ died for us."

The reasons for which Christ, our Priest and propitiatory Sacrifice, had to be not only a man but also the Son of God — God in truth and by nature — have been set forth by Athanasius and Irenaeus elsewhere.[156] Indeed, since Christ, our Mediator and Priest, is the person placed between God, who rages against sin, and our human kind, which is under the penalty of sin and God's wrath, so that He may satisfy God's justice, bear God's wrath against sin, intercede for us, and apply His merits to believers, it is necessary that the two natures be personally united in Him.[157] Why? First, the nature of justice demanded that because the human race had sinned, a human being should pay the penalty; for it is written, "The soul that sinneth, the same shall die." [158] Second, unless the weight of human nature assumed by God's Son had received outside support, it would evidently have perished and been reduced to nothing, just as a body not supported by a soul suffers annihilation. Moreover, our High Priest and Redeemer had to be the Son of God because it was to the highest degree appropriate that human nature be restored through the same Word by whom it had been made and endowed at its first creation with God's image, i. e., with light and life.[159] Also, the human race could not have been redeemed and restored, nor could a sufficient λύτρον [ransom] [160] for the sins of men have been paid, if the Redeemer had not been

[155] These emphatic pronouns appear both in our Lat. text and in the Gk. original.

[156] The classic arguments in the ensuing paragraph may be found in such patristic writings as Athanasius' *On the Incarnation* and *Discourses Against the Arians* and Irenaeus' *Against the Heresies.*

[157] Of the personal or hypostatic union the Lutheran dogmatician J. A. Quenstedt (1617—88) writes: "The form of this personal union implies: (a) The participation or communion of one and the same person, 1 Tim. 2:5; (b) the intimate personal and constant mutual presence of the natures, John 1:14; Col. 2:9." (Quoted in Schmid, *The Doctrinal Theology of the Evangelical Lutheran Church,* trans. Hay and Jacobs, 5th ed., p. 306)

[158] Ezek. 18:4, 20.

[159] Cf. John 1:1-4, 9, 10.

[160] See above, note 85.

God as well as man. For it was necessary not only that so great a penalty for sins be paid but also that such obedience be rendered that it would merit our receiving as a gift true knowledge of God, the Holy Spirit, righteousness, life, and everlasting joy; and the only ἀντάλλαγμα [exchange][161] which can accomplish this is the obedience of God's Son. And no other being would have been able to sustain and overcome the wrath of God and the curse of the Law, bruise the head of the serpent[162] (that is, destroy the works of the devil), take away sin and death, and restore righteousness and eternal life. Furthermore, since the High Priest is officially responsible for revealing and teaching to men the hidden will of God and redemptive wisdom brought forth from the bosom of the Father, and since "no man knoweth the Father save the Son, and he to whom the Son hath willed to reveal Him,"[163] it is essential that a priest ἐξαγγελτικός [with power to proclaim][164] the Gospel be the Son of God. Lastly, because it is characteristic only of divine nature and Emmanuel to be everywhere present in the church, to examine the thoughts of human hearts, to distinguish hypocrisy from true faith, to hearken to the sorrows and longings of those who pray, and to carry out the other functions of a Mediator, we have here clear reasons why the High Priest and Mediator of the church has had to be not just man but true God as well.

The *exterior motivating cause*[165] — or cause προκαταρκτική

161 In the NT this word appears only in the well-known question, "What shall a man give in exchange for his soul?" (Matt. 16:26, Mark 8:37). Cf. Ruth 4:7 (LXX). The centrality of the doctrine of exchange in Christianity has nowhere been better expressed than in the poems, novels, and theological writings of the contemporary British author Charles Williams (d. 1945).

162 Gen. 3:15.

163 Matt. 11:27.

164 This adjective is formed by adding the suffix -τικος, meaning "capable of/fit for" (G-G 188) to the verb ἐξαγγέλλω. The latter contains the root of the NT word for Gospel, and in classical Gk. the noun ἐξάγγελος referred to a messenger who brought out news *from within* (in Sophocles, for example, ἄγγελοι told news from a distance, but ἐξάγγελοι told what was doing behind the scenes). Ἐξαγγέλλω occurs only once in the NT (1 Peter 2:9).

165 On the meaning of "exterior cause," see above, note 154.

[capable of beginning something beforehand] [166] — which led God the Son to become a victim in our behalf was the fall of the first human beings, Adam and Eve; the sin which proceeded from it; and the pitiable condemnation of the whole human race — a race which God's Son was utterly unwilling to have perish. Rom. 4:25: "Christ was delivered for our offenses. . . ." Is. 53:5,6: "He was wounded for our transgressions, He was bruised for our iniquities; the chastisement of our peace was upon Him; and with His stripes we are healed. All we like sheep have gone astray; and the Lord hath laid on Him the iniquity of us all."

The *instrumental and external efficient cause* [167] of the sacrifice and death of Christ are the demons, and the impious Jews who desired to remove and to destroy this teacher who was pointing up their sins.

The *material* element *in which* [168] Christ's sacrifice and sufferings took place was not only the external members of His body which were pierced with nails but especially His soul, which experienced the terrible wrath of God against all of the sin of all mankind; the indescribable pain which arose in His heart from the consciousness of God's wrath and the fear of death; and the admirable humiliation and restraint of His divine nature, which did not put forth its godly power. [169]

The *nature* [170] of Christ's sacrifice is the wonderful obedience and humiliation of the Son of God, who, because of His tremendous

166 As above (note 164), a use of the -τικος suffix with a verb form (here προκατάρχομαι).

167 "*Instrumental cause,* an instrument or tool serving as a subordinate cause; a cause without initiative in the start of action, but applied and directed as a help to its efforts and purpose by a principal agent, and influencing the product chiefly according to the form and intention of the principal." (Wuellner, *Dictionary of Scholastic Philosophy,* p. 19.) Cf. Luther's expression that the devil is ultimately "God's devil." For the meaning of "efficient cause," see above, note 70.

168 On the *materia in qua* concept, see note 77 above.

169 Cf. Erasmus and Colet's debate on the nature of Christ's agony and humiliation in Gethsemane (letters 108—111 in P. S. Allen's edition of Erasmus' *Epistolae*).

170 Lat., *forma.* See above, note 82.

love for the human race, willingly subjected Himself to the eternal Father, and, out of true reverence and His love for God's justice and the salvation of men, endured the wrath of God and the curse poured out upon Him, the bitterest torments of soul and body, and, finally, death itself. Phil. 2:8: "He humbled Himself and became obedient unto death, even the death of the cross." Heb. 5:7,8: "He was heard in that He feared, and though He were a Son, yet obeyed He God in the things which He suffered. . . ." Rom. 5:19: "As by one man's disobedience many were made sinners, so by the obedience of One shall many be made righteous."

The chief *end and result* of the sacrifice of Christ is the redemption and salvation of the human race. Only this sacrifice of God's Son, our Lord Christ, offered up for us on the altar of the cross, secured on the one hand liberation from those saddest and gravest evils — sin, death, the wrath of God, the curse of the Law, the tyranny of the devil, and eternal damnation — and, on the other, those noblest and greatest benefits of all (surely more worth seeking than all the good things in the whole world) — reconciliation with God, righteousness, the Holy Spirit, the renewal of our entire nature, and ultimately eternal life and glory. In all evangelical teaching, but especially in the Gospel and Epistle [171] of John, and in Paul's letters to the Romans, Galatians, Ephesians, Hebrews, etc., there is particular concern to recount and convey these truths. The leading passages, however, are John 3:14-16; Heb. 9:28; Matt. 26:28; Rom. 3:24, 25; and 1 Peter 4:1, 2;[172] 2:24.

The *cognates* [173] of the sacrifice of Christ pertain not to its merit and efficacy, but to its form, i. e., to anguish in some degree parallel with it. Thus the analogs of Christ's passion and death are

[171] Chytraeus probably thinks especially of 1 John, but he may simply be using a collective singular to refer to all three Johannine letters in the NT.

[172] Chytraeus translates "Christ who hath suffered in the flesh hath made sin to cease, that we . . .," instead of "He [i. e., any one] that hath suffered in the flesh hath ceased from sin, that he . . ." (AV). Our author's rendering treats the πέπαυται in the passage as a causative; however, the middle voice of this verb does not have that sense, though the active does. It should be pointed out that Chytraeus' version, in spite of involving a faulty point of grammar, is consistent with the context of these verses and with NT doctrine in general.

[173] Cf. the text at note 101.

the sufferings and afflictions of all the saints,[174] who must be conformed to the image of God's Son hanging on the cross and undergoing death if they would participate also in like glory and resurrection. Rom. 8:17: "We are joint heirs with Christ; if so be that we suffer with Him, that we may be also glorified together with Him." 2 Cor. 4:10: "Always bearing about in the body the dying of the Lord Jesus that the life also of Jesus might be made manifest in our body." 1 Peter 2:21: "Christ suffered for us, leaving us an example, that we [175] should follow His steps. . . ." Paul also described this kind of sacrifice in Rom. 12:1 ("Present your bodies a living sacrifice, holy, acceptable unto God, which is your reasonable service"), and in Rom. 8:36 ("For Thy sake we are killed all the day long; we are accounted as sheep for the slaughter").[176]

Under this topic of the cognates or analogs of Christ's propitiatory sacrifice can also be discussed all its types and representations which God set forth in such a manifold way in the Old Testament. He did this in order that there might continually be signs, reminders, and occasions for teaching the people about the future sacrifice of God's Son, which alone expiates and takes away the sin of the world. Such shadows and representations were Abel's lamb, the sacrifice of Isaac,[177] the Passover lamb, the brass serpent lifted up in the wilderness,[178] and, finally, all the burnt offerings and sacrifices — the sin offering, the trespass offering, and others — which the Levitical priests daily offered to God.

C. *Misconceptions Concerning the Sacrifice of Christ*

Here are included all the errors by which in every age the doctrine of Christ's sacrifice has been distorted as to nature and true value. For example, Basilides, Cerdo, and the Marcionites supposed that Christ was sacrificed, suffered, and died for us, not really

---

[174] As in evangelical writings generally, the word "saint" here is equivalent to "believer" (one justified by grace through faith); it does not refer to one whom a church has designated as an especially holy person.

[175] Gk. and AV have "ye." The best reading of the Gk. has the second person throughout the verse.

[176] Here Paul quotes Ps. 44:22.

[177] In connection with these typological interpretations, see Patrick Fairbairn's great work, *The Typology of Scripture*, reprint ed. (Grand Rapids: Zondervan, n. d.), 2 vols. in 1.

[178] Num. 21:6-9; John 3:14-16.

but δοκήσει, that is, only seemingly or in appearance.[179] Some imagine that Christ by His sacrifice offered satisfaction only for original sin and for transgressions committed prior to one's first conversion to God, but that everyone must expiate subsequent sins by his own works, almsgiving, pilgrimages, fasts, masses, and the like. Others teach that by His sacrifice Christ merited for us only a first infusion of grace, and that, after this infusion has occurred, we are justified and made heirs of eternal life, not solely because of Christ's sacrifice appropriated by faith alone but partly because of Christ and partly because of the fulfillment of the Law accomplished in a state of grace. And others, as we shall see a little later, think that Christ's sacrifice is applied to us through the sacrifice of the Mass.

[179] Basilides (ca. 130) is representative of the Egyptian variety of Gnosticism; his views were popularized by Valentinus, the most influential Gnostic teacher. According to Irenaeus, Basilides taught, *inter alia,* that Christ "suffered not, but a certain Simon, a Cyrenian, was impressed to bear his cross for him; and Simon was crucified in ignorance and error, having been transfigured by him, that men should suppose him to be Jesus, while Jesus himself took on the appearance of Simon and stood by and mocked them" (quoted in Henry Bettenson, ed., *Documents of the Christian Church* [New York and London: Oxford University Press, 1950], p. 51). On Cerdo, J. L. Neve writes: "It is known that Marcion was more or less influenced by the Syrian Gnostic Cerdo" (*A History of Christian Thought,* I [Philadelphia: Muhlenberg Press, 1946], 57). Whether one classes Marcion as a Gnostic or not, there is no doubt that in common with the Gnostics he held a Docetic view of Christ.

IV

THE PRIESTHOOD OF ALL BELIEVERS

A. *The Scriptural Basis of the Doctrine*

And so the Son of God, our Lord and Redeemer Jesus Christ, by the immeasurable goodness and wondrous plan of the entire Godhead, was constituted the eternal High Priest of the church, revealed the Gospel, interceded for the human race, which had fallen into sin and death, and presented Himself as an offering and sacrifice to God — all this in order that He might make us priests emancipated from the slavery of sin and death and provide us with free access to our God and Father, Christ Himself as High Priest and Mediator leading the way. To us, then, God granted[z] the right of teaching the Gospel, praying for ourselves and others, presenting the sacrifices and victims commanded by Him, and carrying out the other duties of priests who have been consecrated to God. As John says:[180] "Christ loved us and washed us from our sins in His own blood and hath made us kings and priests unto our[181] God and Father." Note also 1 Peter 2:4, 5: "Ye were redeemed with the precious blood of Christ, as of a lamb without blemish,[182] to whom coming, as unto a living stone, ye also as lively stones should be built up[183] a spiritual house, an holy priesthood, to offer up spiritual sacrifices acceptable to God by

---

[180] Rev. 1:5, 6.

[181] The Gk. and AV have "unto God and His Father."

[182] The quotation to this point is from 1 Peter 1:18, 19.

[183] The Gk. οἰχοδομεῖσϑε can morphologically be either a present imperative or a present indicative. Chytraeus takes it as the former and renders it by a Latin subjunctive; the AV takes it as the latter and translates "are built up." The AV rendering is to be preferred, for, as Hort argues: "It is remarkable that St. Peter habitually uses the aorist for his imperatives, even when we might expect the present; the only exceptions (two or three) are preceded by words removing all ambiguity" (quoted by J. H. A. Hart in EG V, 55).

Jesus Christ"; and a little later [184] we read: "Ye are a chosen generation, a royal priesthood, an holy nation, a peculiar people, that ye should show forth the praises of Him who hath called you out of darkness into His marvelous light."

In the New Testament, consequently, priesthood is not the prerogative of one particular order of men set apart from layfolk by outward anointing, tonsure, dress, and function, but it belongs equally to all Christians and is the common property of all. For all Christians, because they have been born again of water and of the Spirit [185] and believe in Christ, are priests who have been divinely ordained in order that they might confess and teach the truth concerning God and our Redeemer Jesus Christ, pray God for themselves and others through their trust in Christ as Mediator, and present to God spiritual sacrifices and offerings.[aa] The latter consist not of dead animals but of a real, living response kindled by the Holy Spirit in the heart, a knowledge and celebration of the gracious benefits shown forth to us in Christ, true supplication, thanksgiving, confession, preaching the divine doctrine, joyful obedience with regard to all of God's commands, and every action — whether in this life or after it [186] — whose purpose is the worship of God. All of the preceding are sacrifices of praise, or spiritual offerings, which are living, holy, and pleasing to God through Christ Jesus.

The testimonies which I am about to give will show clearly that the New Testament priesthood and sacrifices are common to all Christians; that in the New Testament there is no ceremonial or visible priesthood in the hands of a particular order and distinct from the priesthood of the people; that priests are not now created or ordained by men but are born of God through His Word and Baptism; and that therefore all Christians have equal priestly dignity

[184] 1 Peter 2:9.

[185] Cf. John 3:3-5.

[186] The belief that spiritual sacrifice exists in heaven is consistent not only with the testimony of the canonical Scriptures (note especially the Book of Revelation) but also with the high theological and literary tradition which from the time of Pseudo-Dionysius has seen the heavens filled with seraphim, cherubim, thrones, dominions, virtues, powers, princedoms, archangels, and angels, as well as with the saints — and all offering sacrifices of praise to God continually.

and the same right to carry out sacerdotal functions before God and offer the sacrifices which He has commanded. We shall center our attention on verses from 1 Peter 1 and 2.

"Ye were redeemed with the precious blood of Christ, as of a lamb without blemish, and were born again, not of corruptible seed but of incorruptible, by the Word of God, who [187] *liveth and abideth forever."* [188] Since all men are conceived in sin [189] and are born into slavery as children of wrath and of eternal death and (so to speak) as priests and property of the devil,[190] they could not by any human ability free themselves from such great evils or from their captivity to so fierce an enemy — much less become sons and priests of God and heirs of a heavenly life and kingdom — had Christ as the Lamb of God not paid the penalty, and they not been reborn, i. e., been given new life and righteousness through the same Son of God, the Λόγος, or Word of God, who lives forever. God's regeneration of men, in order that they might be made His sons and priests, is accomplished through two means:[191] (1) the Gospel of Christ, or the Word of the living God, which we receive by faith and through which the very Son of God, as the eternal Λόγος, together with the Holy Spirit, act in an efficacious manner; and (2) the sacrament of Baptism. Thus Peter says here, "Ye were born again by the Word of the living God," and Christ says elsewhere,[192] "Except a man be born again of water and of the Holy Spirit, he cannot enter into the kingdom of God."

[187] The Gk. may also be translated "which"; the latter is used in the AV. Chytraeus and the Vulgate agree here, and J. H. A. Hart writes: "The rendering of the Vulgate, *per verbum dei vivi et permanentis,* is supported by Dan. vi. 26 (αὐτὸς γάρ ἐστιν θεὸς μένων καὶ ζῶν) and supports St. Peter's argument: earthly relationships must perish with all flesh and its glory; spiritual kinship abides, because it is based on the relation of the kinsfolk to *God living and abiding"* (EG V, 53).

[188] 1 Peter 1:18, 19, 23.

[189] A reference to Ps. 51:5.

[190] Cf. John 8:44.

[191] With these remarks on the means of grace, cf. Regin Prenter's presentation of Luther's doctrine of the Holy Spirit: *Spiritus Creator,* trans. J. M. Jensen (Philadelphia: Muhlenberg Press, 1953), chap. 2 ("The Means Used by the Holy Spirit," with subsections "The Spirit and the Word" and "The Spirit and the Sacraments").

[192] John 3:5. "Born again" (rather than simply "born") and "Holy Spirit" (rather than simply "Spirit") are Vulgate readings.

"Wherefore" [193] (i. e., because through regeneration the old nature dies and sin is destroyed within you and the new life is begun in you by Christ, the Word of the living God), *"laying aside all malice and all guile and hypocrisies and envies and all evil speakings, as newborn babes"* (or God's infants, regenerated by Him through a spiritual birth, and strangers to all selfish preferment, guile, and deceit — cf. Matt. 18:1-4) *"desire the sincere milk of the Word"* (that is, pure doctrine and a life of innocence, or faith and obedience toward God — not in pretense or ignorance but in sincerity, truth, and understanding, with knowledge of and trust in the Mediator, and for the purpose of worshiping God) *"that ye may grow thereby"* (for it is not enough to have begun well; one must advance and mature into a perfect man — Eph. 4: 11-15) *"if so be ye have tasted that the Lord"* (i. e., Jesus Christ) *"is gracious"* (Ps. 34:8; you will indeed strive the more zealously to advance along this path of pure religion because you have already known the taste of true acquaintance with God and of the benefits of Jesus Christ). *"To whom coming"* by faith, *"as unto a living Stone"* (that is, the firm and immovable Foundation of our salvation and of the whole church, and the source of everlasting life — 1 Cor. 3:11; John 5—7), *"disallowed indeed of men"* (unbelievers, and especially the Jewish architects who should have built the church on this Foundation — Ps. 118:22; Matt. 21:42) *"but chosen of God and precious"* (to all who believe in Christ and trust entirely in Him for righteousness, salvation, and eternal life — Is. 28:16; Acts 4:10-12), *"ye also, as lively stones"* (i. e., true and living members of the church, or living temples of God), *"should be built up"* [194] (so that, specifically, God may through His Word create in you believers a real, vital knowledge of Him and of our Lord Jesus Christ, true righteousness and eternal life, free from sin and death — a building process begun in this life and to be completed throughout eternity [195]) *"a spiritual house"* (that is, abodes and temples of God, not physical dwellings or edifices of stone, or houses furnished only with philosophical doctrine and morality, but

[193] Here begins Chytraeus' phrase-by-phrase exegesis of 1 Peter 2:1-9.

[194] See above, note 183.

[195] The text has *externitate* misprinted for *(a)eternitate* here.

spiritual homes where God Himself lives and thus communicates Himself and the highest and best that He has — life, light, wisdom, and righteousness — and brings hearts into conformity and harmony with Himself),[bb] *"an holy priesthood"* (i. e., holy priests, sanctified by the unique sacrifice of the High Priest; purified and cleansed from sin before God; and consecrated and anointed by God's Holy Spirit — that they may serve God with virtuous mind, reverent tongue, and a life of full obedience), *"to offer up spiritual sacrifices"* (not the carcasses of animals, as the Mosaic priests offered, nor simply the respectable and ethical works of natural morality, such as the pagans offer, but the pure, inner affections of the heart, kindled by the Holy Spirit — viz., true fear and love of God, faith, thanksgiving, confession, patience, and other good works — with true knowledge of Christ as Mediator providing the illumination, and with the worship of God as the goal), *"acceptable to God by Jesus Christ"* (we shall discuss this more fully a little later).

"Wherefore also it is contained in the Scripture" (Is. 28:16), *"Behold, I lay in Sion a chief Cornerstone"* (meaning Christ, the immovable Foundation of the church, who joins and holds together two walls — the Jews and the Gentiles, uniting them in one church to form a community with a single faith and eternal salvation), *"elect, precious; and he that believeth on Him shall not be confounded"* (referring to the person who will with firm faith lean upon Christ as the only Rock of our salvation, center on Him all trust for his righteousness and salvation, come to a sound acknowledgment of Christ's person and benefits, and be fully convinced that his sins have been remitted and righteousness and eternal life given to him because of Christ). *"Unto you therefore which believe He is precious; but unto them which do not believe"*[196] (here are meant the unbelieving church leaders among the Jewish people, and all others who had the responsibility to establish the church on Christ as the Foundation, and to build up and encourage in the minds of their hearers the conviction that they were freed from sin and death and granted eternal life because of the unique Christ and Him alone), *"the Stone which the builders disallowed, the same is made the Head of the corner"* (i. e., the chief Cornerstone, conjoining the church of the Jews and of the Gentiles — Ps. 118:22; Acts 4:10, 11; Matt. 21:42) *"and a Stone of stumbling and a Rock*

---

[196] The AV "which be disobedient" is based on a less adequate MS reading.

92

of offense" (Is. 8:13-15), *"even to them which stumble at the Word,
unbelieving;*[197] *whereunto also they were appointed. But ye"* (Gentiles and Jews who by faith embrace the Gospel and are priests
and sons of God by virtue of a divine birth) *"are a chosen generation"* (you are the noblest and most eminent members of the
human race, for you have been chosen from among all men by the
immense goodness and mercy of God[198] that you may be God's
beloved people, His personal possession, His children, heirs of
every heavenly blessing, and heralds[199] of the divine glory in this
life and throughout eternity — Ex. 19:4-6), *"a royal priesthood"*
(that is, royal priests — kings, lords, and victors over sin, death,
and the devil, and heirs of life and of a celestial kingdom; and at
the same time priests proclaiming and celebrating God's benefits
and glories).

The royal priesthood concept is also presented by John. Rev.
1:6: *"Christ hath made us kings and priests unto our*[200] *God and
Father."* Rev. 5:9, 10: *"They sung a new song unto the Lamb: . . .
Thou wast slain and hast redeemed us to God by Thy blood out of
every kindred and tongue and people and nation and hast made us
unto our God kings and priests; and we shall reign on the earth."*
Rev. 20:6: *"Blessed and holy is he that hath part in the first resurrection"* (in which a man is justified by Christ — freed from his

---

[197] The AV translation, "being disobedient," is a more secure rendering of
ἀπειθοῦντες; however, "since, in the view of the early Christians, the supreme disobedience was a refusal to believe their gospel, ἀ. may be restricted
in some passages to the mng. *disbelieve, be an unbeliever.* This sense, though
greatly disputed (it is not found outside our lit.), seems most probable in
John 3:36; Acts 14:2; 19:9; Rom. 15:31, and only slightly less prob.
in . . . 1 Peter 2:8" (A-G 82).

[198] From the outset, Lutherans have held to the doctrine of the divine election of the saved, while refusing to accept the Calvinistic "double predestination" which makes God responsible also for the damnation of the lost.
It may thus be said that what Lutheran theology loses in logical consistency
to Calvinism (and to its opposite, Arminio-Pelagianism), it gains in faithful, inductive exegesis of the Scriptural revelation. See the excellent article
"Predestination" in *Lutheran Cyclopedia,* ed. E. L. Lueker (St. Louis: Concordia, 1954), pp. 839—841 (including full bibliography).

[199] *Praeco* was used by Commodianus (5th C.) to mean "a prophet," and
Irenaeus, etc., employed *praecono* in the sense of the Gk. κηρύσσω, "proclaim/preach" (SGLL 312).

[200] See note 181.

natural slavery to sins and eternal death — through conversion to God and faith; Eph. 2:5 states that "even when we were dead in sins, He [201] hath quickened us together with Him" by forgiving us all our sins, and Col. 2:12 says that "in Christ [202] ye are risen through the faith of the operation of God" [203]); *"on such the second death"* (eternal damnation) *"hath no power, but they shall be priests of God and of Christ and shall reign with Him."* These Johannine verses clearly harmonize with the passage from Peter and serve to elucidate it.

Now Peter continues his description of the priesthood of Christians as follows: [204] "Ye are *an holy nation"* (i. e., a race cleansed from sin and consecrated to God by the blood of Christ, that henceforth you may be subject to God rather than to wicked practices and may manifest His glory), *"a peculiar people"* (that is, a people won and redeemed by Christ and thus a most precious κειμήλιον [treasure] and most beloved personal possession of God — Ex. 19:4-6; Deut. 7:6-8; Eph. 1:4-14; Titus 2:14); *"that ye should show forth the praises of Him who hath called you out of darkness into His marvelous light."* This latter, indeed, is the first and foremost duty of the priests' office — with thankful mind and voice to acknowledge, confess, and proclaim and preach to others God's grace, goodness, mercy, truth, and all the benefits which He has given to us through and because of His Son Jesus Christ slain and risen for us. We should preach this in order that they too may discern God's mighty acts and benefits given to us in Christ and embrace and worship the God who through the Gospel has called us out of the darkness of spiritual ignorance, sin, death, and eternal damnation into His marvelous light. There, where the gloom and darkness of error and doubt are dispersed, a true knowledge of God and our Redeemer Jesus Christ illumines their minds, revives

[201] I. e., God; the "Him" in the quotation refers to Christ.

[202] Chytraeus thus takes the ἐν ᾧ in this verse to refer to Christ rather than to Baptism and in doing so follows Chrysostom and Luther, over against Calvin (and, incidentally, most modern exegetes). See EG III, 525, 526.

[203] It will be evident from the preceding interpretation of the expression "first resurrection" that Chytraeus does not see in Rev. 20 a futurist-millenarian description of the end of the age.

[204] 1 Peter 2:9.

their hearts and wills dead in trespasses and sins, and, with the abolishment of sin and death, stimulates in them a new righteousness and a God-pleasing life.

B. The Privileges and Responsibilities of Christian Priests [205]

The above passage from Peter and the three testimonies from John included with it are the only ones in the entire New Testament which expressly mention a priesthood and priests other than Christ and His high priesthood, and it is evident that these verses pertain equally to all Christians and confer the title and honor, the name and right of priests, not upon a particular order of men but upon every reborn person. The universality of this priesthood is also shown by the characteristic functions of these priests, which are: to offer sacrifices to God; to approach Him, i. e., to pray for oneself and others; to confess and teach God's Word; to pass judgment on all doctrines and spirits; [206] to baptize and administer the Eucharist; to bind and loose sins; [207] etc. That all these activities are appropriate and common to all Christians and are equally required of all believers, lay and clerical, is manifestly clear from the testimonies about to be given out of Holy Scripture.

First, commands to sacrifice are well known which apply to all Christians alike. Examples are Rom. 12:1; 1 Peter 2:5; Ps. 50:14; 51:17; 4:5; Heb. 13:15, 16. Thus all Christians have not only an equal right but also a most emphatic command to offer sacrifices to God; and everyone admits that only priests are under such an obligation.

A little later I shall present a more detailed treatment of these particular sacrifices, but now I am going to cite passages dealing with the second characteristic priestly function, namely, that of approaching God — praying and interceding to Him for oneself and others. The following testimonies will, like those just given,

[205] With the material in this section, cf. T. A. Kantonen, *Resurgence of the Gospel* (Philadelphia: Muhlenberg Press, 1948), chap. 4; T. A. Kantonen, *A Theology for Christian Stewardship* (Philadelphia: Muhlenberg Press, 1956), chap. 7; R. C. H. Lenski, *Kings and Priests* (Burlington, Iowa: Lutheran Literary Board, 1927), *passim;* and L. W. Spitz, "The Universal Priesthood of Believers," in *The Abiding Word,* ed. Theodore Laetsch, I (St. Louis: Concordia, 1946), 321—341.

[206] Cf. 1 John 4:1-3.

[207] Matt. 16:19; 18:15-18; John 20:23.

demonstrate that the right of priesthood in the New Testament is the common property of all Christians. Eph. 3:12: "In Christ we have boldness and access to God [208] with confidence through our faith in Him." [209] Therefore Christ Himself laid down for all Christians a pattern of approach to God — the Lord's Prayer — and added a requirement for and a promise of being heard: "Ask and ye shall receive"; [210] "Whatsoever ye shall ask the Father in My name, He will give it you." [211] Note also Christ's words in Luke 11:13 and 18:1; and cf. Ps. 50:15; 1 Tim. 2:1, 2; and Heb. 4:16.

In the third place, all Christians, by the very fact that they hear the Gospel and embrace it by faith, i. e., believe in Christ, are taught of God, and have the right to teach others and to confess, preach, and propagate the Gospel and Christ's benefits. This is shown by the following verses: Ps. 116:10 and 2 Cor. 4:13; Col. 3:16; 1 Peter 2:9; 1 Cor. 11:26 ("As often as ye eat this bread and drink this cup, ye do proclaim [212] the Lord's death till He come"). This latter verse proves that not only the ministers who distribute the sacrament, but all those who partake of the Lord's Supper have the privilege and responsibility of proclaiming the death of our Lord Jesus Christ, that is, of teaching the benefits which Christ has provided in freeing us by His death from the dark kingdom of sin and death and restoring us into the marvelous light of righteousness and everlasting life. Also note Ps. 51:13, 15; 1 Cor. 14:31: "Ye may all prophesy one by one" (i. e., interpret the prophetic Scripture) "that all may learn and all may be comforted"; Ps. 149:5-7: "This glory is for all His saints.[213] Let the high praises of God be in their mouth, and a two-edged sword" (the divine Word — Heb. 4:12) "in their hand, to execute vengeance upon the heathen. . . ."

208 Chytraeus adds "to God" for the sake of clarification.

209 The AV "by the faith of Him" (subjective rather than objective genitive) is a less adequate rendering of the Gk. (see EG III, 310).

210 Matt. 7:7, 8; 21:22; Luke 11:9, 10; John 16:24.

211 John 16:23.

212 In this verse the Lat. employs the verb *annuncio*, "*proclaim* the Lord's death till He come"; this is a much better rendering of the Gk. καταγγέλλω than the AV "show."

213 A more literal rendering of the Heb. is: "The saints are joyful in glory" (cf. Franz Delitzsch, *Biblical Commentary on the Psalms,* trans. David Eaton, III [London: Hodder and Stoughton, 1889], 422).

Fourth, all Christians are commanded to pass judgment on all doctrines and spirits, to approve right doctrine, and to recognize and reject false dogmas and the teachers of them. This John declares, addressing all the faithful: "Believe not every spirit, but try the spirits" (dogmas and doctors) "whether they are of God" (1 John 4:1); "Ye have an unction from the Holy One, which teacheth you all things." [214] See also 1 Thess. 5:20, 21; John 10:27, 5; Matt. 7:15, 16; 16:6; [215] and note Matt. 23:2, 3: [216] "The scribes and the Pharisees sit in Moses' seat; all whatsoever they bid you observe" (that is to say, everything consistent with Moses' teaching), "that observe and do; but do not ye after their works."

Fifth, as Christ asserts in a lengthy saying, Matt. 18:15-18, all Christians alike have the keys, or power to bind and loose sins, i. e., to declare sins remitted or retained.

In the sixth place, the privilege of receiving and administering the sacraments of Baptism and the Lord's Supper also applies to all members of the church, not just to sacrificing priests who have been anointed and tonsured. The truth of this is shown by the fact that even [cc] women are permitted, in case of necessity, to baptize — to administer the life-giving Word of God by which man is regenerated and freed from sin, death, and the power of the devil.[217] And [dd] with regard to the Lord's Supper, Christ says to all Christians: "This do in remembrance of Me."

We have definitely established, then, that the priesthood of the New Testament and all the sacerdotal functions connected with it are equally common to all Christians and that the New Testament sets forth no particular priestly order distinct from the laity — that, to the contrary, all alike who have been reborn by the Holy Spirit through God's Word and believe in Christ are priests and truly spiritual persons. Thus Paul calls the ministers of the church — those in charge of preaching the Word and administering the

[214] 1 John 2:20, 27; cf. John 14:26.

[215] The text has Matt. 19 for Matt. 16 — undoubtedly a printer's error.

[216] The text rubrication incorrectly gives Matt. 13, which may be another *mendum typographicum.*

[217] A point worth careful consideration in present-day discussions as to the legitimacy and propriety of ordaining women to the Gospel ministry.

sacraments — not "priests" or "spiritual persons"[218] (for these desig-
nations apply equally to all Christians ruled by the Holy Spirit) but
"ministers," "pastors," "bishops," "deacons," "elders," "stewards,"[219]
"servants," etc.

C. The Professional Ministry

Now[ee] although the New Testament priesthood is universal,
no one in the public assembly of the church should appropriate
or discharge on his own authority this right which is the common
property of all. Rather, some men who are particularly fitted for
the task are to be chosen and called by general vote to carry out
publicly — in the name of all who have the same right — the
functions of teaching, binding and loosing,[220] and administering
the sacraments. For necessary to the public execution of the priestly
office of instructing, consoling, exhorting, denouncing sins, judging
controversies over doctrine, etc., is a thorough knowledge of Christian theology, a faculty for teaching, skill in languages, speaking
ability, and other gifts, and these are not equally manifest in all
whom the Holy Spirit has regenerated; therefore those who lack
these talents rightly yield[221] their privileges to others better endowed than themselves.

[218] Cf. such Pauline passages as 1 Cor. 2:15; 3:1; 14:37; Gal. 6:1. Note
the semantic problem in the German language, where the noun *Geistliche*,
from the adj. *geistlich* ("spiritual"), does not mean "spiritual person" in
general but "clergyman/minister/divine/priest."

[219] In 1 Cor. 4:1, 2 and Titus 1:7. The Gk. word is οἰκονόμος, the Lat.,
dispensator.

[220] See point five in the section immediately preceding.

[221] Lat., *concedunt*. We have here in Chytraeus a clear statement of the
Uebertragungslehre, or "transference theory," of the ministry — a position
held by Luther but opposed by such orthodox Lutheran theologians as
Chemnitz, Gerhard, and Hollaz. The fact that Chytraeus supports the theory
demonstrates the lack of preciseness in G. H. Gerberding's assertion that
"it was not, however, the doctrine of the Lutheran dogmaticians of the sixteenth and seventeenth centuries" (*The Lutheran Pastor*, 7th ed. [Minneap-
olis: Augsburg, 1915], p. 78), and "this transference theory is not held by
our older theologians" (ibid., p. 82). It should be noted, in fairness to
Chytraeus, that the "transfer" here described does not necessarily undercut
the doctrine of the priesthood of all believers or the practice of lay stewardship, for the transfer is neither complete nor arbitrary. A layman trans-
fers only those priestly functions (a) which if exercised indiscriminately

For God is not the author of disorder and ἀκαταστασία [confusion] but of order and peace.[222] Therefore, so that all things might be done εὐσχημόνως [decently] and in order[223] and to prevent barbaric confusion and a Cyclopean ἀγορὰ ἐν ᾗ ἀκούει οὐδεὶς οὐδὲν οὐδενός [assembly where nobody heeds anybody in anything][224] from existing in the church, Paul himself established a particular order of vocation[225] and commands that this ministry be committed to suitable and faithful men who should teach others.[226] In Titus 1:5-9 and 1 Tim. 3:1-7, he sets forth at length the qualifications of the bishop or minister of the Gospel who has the duty of performing and administering sacerdotal functions in the public assembly of the church. Paul does not differentiate bishops, presbyters, and pastors; he assigns precisely equal dignity of rank and the same office to presbyters and to bishops — and it is in fact clear that there were many such in individual towns. In Acts 20, Paul says to the presbyters of the church at Ephesus whom he has called to him: "Take heed unto yourselves and to all the flock, over the which the Holy Ghost hath made you bishops, to feed the church of God."[227] Note also Phil. 1:1; Titus 1:5-7; 1 Peter 5:1, 2;[228] etc.

by all would produce confusion and disorder in the church (e. g., the administration of the sacraments) and (b) for which he personally lacks the required ability and training (e. g., in most instances, the preparation and delivery of sermons).

222 1 Cor. 14:33, where the Gk. word is used.

223 1 Cor. 14:40, where the Gk. word is employed.

224 Alluding to Euripides' *Cyclops*, 120. Odysseus asks Silenus whether the Cyclopes have a ruler; he replies: νομάδες· ἀκούει δ' οὐδὲν οὐδεὶς οὐδενός ("They are shepherds, and nobody heeds anybody in anything"). Cf. Homer's *Odyssey*, ix. 114: "Each gives the law to his children and wives, and they do not heed one another."

225 Lat., *ordinem vocationis certum*.

226 2 Tim. 2:2.

227 In Acts 20:17 the term πρεσβύτερος ("presbyter/elder") is employed; in v. 28 here quoted ἐπίσκοπος ("overseer/bishop") is used to refer to those holding the same office.

228 The verb translated "taking the oversight" in the AV of 1 Peter 5:2 is the Gk. ἐπισκοπέω; it is, however, omitted in the best manuscript readings of the verse. In quoting the verse, Chytraeus gives "flock of Christ" for "flock of God."

Later, by human authority, ranks were established among the ministers and bishops, and within the presbyterate there appeared the ostiary, the psalmist, the lector, the exorcist, the acolyte, the subdeacon, the deacon, and the priest.[229] One bishop — or overseer, or superintendent [230] — was placed in charge of many presbyters or pastors of individual churches.

An archbishop, or metropolitan, came to exercise authority over the bishops. In Germany, there are six of these — the archbishops of Mainz, Cologne, Trier, Magdeburg, Salzburg, and Bremen. Of these there belong to the archbishop of Mainz the sees of Strassburg, Speyer, Worms, Würzburg, Augsburg, Constance, Chur, Eichstätt, Hildesheim, Halberstadt, Paderborn, and Verden; to the archbishop of Cologne the sees of Münster, Minden, Osnabrück, Utrecht, and Liége; to the archbishop of Trier the sees of Metz, Toul, and Verdun; to the archbishop of Magdeburg the sees of Merseburg, Naumberg, Brandenburg, and Havelberg; to the archbishop of Salzburg the sees of Passau, Vienna, Trent, Brixen, Gurk, and Freising. The sees of Lübeck, Ratzeburg, and Schwerin have been exempted from the archbishop of Bremen in Saxony.[231] In upper Germany [232] the bishoprics of Bamberg, Regensburg, and Basel

[229] *Ostiarii* (porters), lectors, exorcists, and acolytes comprise the four Minor Orders of the Roman clergy. Until the 12th century, the subdiaconate was included in the Minor Orders. "The four Minor Orders and the Subdiaconate are not Sacraments but merely Sacramentals" (Ludwig Ott, *Fundamentals of Catholic Dogma,* ed. J. C. Bastible, trans. Patrick Lynch [Saint Louis: Herder, 1958], p. 452).

[230] It is worthwhile to remind ourselves of the church organization characteristic of Chytraeus' own time: "Because the Peace of Augsburg had recognized the abolition of episcopal authority in the Protestant territories without stipulating who should exercise it, the Lutheran princes in general appropriated it. . . . Superintendents appointed by the princes supervised the clergy and presided over their synods." (H. J. Grimm, *The Reformation Era* [New York: Macmillan, 1954], p. 484)

[231] Latin place names in the succeeding lists were identified by means of J. G. Th. Graesse's *Orbis Latinus, oder Verzeichnis der wichtigsten lateinischen Orts- und Ländernamen,* 3d ed. by Friedrich Benedict (Berlin: R. C. Schmidt, 1922). A valuable map showing these bishoprics and archbishoprics is that titled, "Kirchliche Einteilung Mittel- und Westeuropas am Ausgang des Mittelalters," in *Neuer Geschichts- und Kulturatlas,* ed. Hans Zeissig, 2d ed. (Frankfurt, etc.: Atlantik-Verlag Paul List, 1954), p. 50.

[232] *Germania superior* was a term used to distinguish Germany proper (especially south Germany, including Austria and Switzerland) from

have similarly been released — and, if I remember rightly,[233] this is true also of Meissen.

In any country the archbishops are responsible to a primate, or patriarch. In Germany this is the archbishop of Magdeburg; in France I think it is the archbishop of Reims;[ff] in Portugal, the archbishop of Braga. In the nearby kingdoms of Scandinavia, about the year 1060, the title of primate of Sweden was conferred upon Aeschylus, the archbishop of Lund, by Pope Nicholas II — which the Swedes, however, never recognized.[234]

This episcopal order and the ranks connected with it are not evil in themselves.[235] They should not be disparaged when they serve to uphold the unity and harmony of the church in true evangelical doctrine and the preservation of Christian discipline and

Germania inferior ("lower Germany," particularly what we today call "the Netherlands/the Low Countries"). *Superior* and *inferior* in these expressions of course refer to altitude.

[233] He does; however, he is in error concerning Vienna, which held an exempt status similar to that of Bamberg, etc.

[234] In naming primates, Chytraeus wrongly gives Magdeburg for Germany (Mainz is correct). With regard to the elevation of Lund to the primacy of Sweden, our author's remarks suffer from some confusion also. By "Aeschylus" he refers to Bishop Eskil(lus) of Lund, who was in fact made primate of Sweden; however, this occurred a century later than Chytraeus indicates — in 1152, to be exact (see *The Catholic Encyclopedia,* V [New York: Appleton, 1909], 538 [art. "Eskil"]; John Wordsworth, *The National Church of Sweden* [London: Mowbray, 1911], p. 107; and P. B. Gams, ed., *Series episcoporum Ecclesiae Catholicae* [Leipzig: Hiersemann, 1931], pp. 330, 332). Thus Nicholas II (pope 1059—61) had nothing to do with the elevation of Lund to the primacy. Our author's remark about a refusal to recognize Nicholas becomes clear when we note that the German bishops attemped to depose him in 1060. "During the course, it would seem, of the summer of the year 1060, 'the chief officials *(rectores)* of the royal court, along with, forsooth, some holy bishops of the Teutonic kingdom, conspiring against the Roman Church, collected a council. Therein, with an audacity wholly incredible, they passed sentence upon the Pope and declared all that he had decreed null and void'" (H. K. Mann, *The Lives of the Popes in the Middle Ages,* VI, 2d ed. [London: Kegan Paul, 1925], 254).

[235] "It is not necessary that human traditions, rites or ceremonies instituted by men, should be alike everywhere." (Augsburg Confession, Art. VII ["Of the Church"]; cf. Art. XV ["Of Ecclesiastical Rites"])

peace; when they maintain and spread right doctrine and reverent worship of God; when they do not claim that they possess the illicit power to interpret Scripture arbitrarily, to establish new articles of faith, to legislate in matters of doctrine and worship; and when they do not assume tyrannical authority over the other members of the church; etc.

V

CHRISTIAN THANK OFFERINGS

A. *What the Concept Signifies*

Inasmuch as our discussion so far has been about the priesthood common to every Christian, we shall now add a few remarks with regard to the New Testament thank offerings [236] of cross-bearing and praise which all Christians alike are to present to God.

God created men, not that they should lead tranquil lives free of all difficulty and responsibility and accomplish nothing [237] but in order that He might communicate Himself and the highest and best that He has — light, wisdom, righteousness, and life — to them, and that they for their part might become like Him, acknowledge His goodness, and worship Him for it. It is therefore necessary that there be certain activities through which God communicates Himself to us in this life and which have as their purpose the worship of God. Such are: the study of the doctrine God has handed down, knowledge of God and of our Lord Jesus Christ, filial reverence toward God, faith, confession, prayer, thanksgiving, the love of God, conformity of heart to His will, joy in God, etc.

---

[236] Lat., *sacrificia eucharistica.* See note 289.

[237] A point deserving serious consideration by the authors and readers of the numerous "peace of mind" publications which constitute a plethora on the religious book market at present. One is reminded of the clerical example provided by Don Abbondio in Alessandro Manzoni's *I Promessi Sposi:* "Don Abbondio was continuously absorbed in thinking about his own peace and quiet, and had not bothered about advantages which were to be enjoyed only at the cost of a good deal of bother and a certain amount of risk. His system consisted chiefly in steering clear of all quarrels, or giving way when he could not avoid them. . . . He denounced those of his brother-clergy who at their own risk took the side of the weak and oppressed against the tyrannical and strong. This he called rushing into a quarrel, or trying to straighten out a dog's leg; he would even say severely that this was getting mixed up with things profane and prejudicing the dignity of their holy office." (*The Betrothed,* trans. Archibald Colquhoun [London: Dent; New York: Dutton, 1956 (Everyman's Library, 999)], pp. 11, 12)

Through these activities a man becomes a temple of God [238] and a worshiper of Him in this life and throughout eternity.

These actions are real and everlasting sacrifices and are common at all times to all priests of God — that is, to all believers — in the Church Triumphant as well as Militant. It is true that the original source of these sacrifices and of the eternal worship of God is the teaching ministry and the preaching of the Gospel, whereby God communicates Himself to us in this life and kindles in us genuine knowledge and worship of Himself; and it is likewise true that this mode of teaching through the ministry will cease after this life. However, practically all other sacrifices — viz., clear knowledge of God and of our Lord Jesus Christ, love of God, joy in the Lord, confession, thanksgiving, worship and glorification of Him, and, finally, complete righteousness and conformity to His will, etc. — these will remain and be perfected throughout eternity, and through them God will communicate His very Self to the blessed.

Now these eternal means of divine worship — these perpetual sacrifices which each person must begin to offer in this life — are not propitiatory. Their purpose is not to merit the remission of sins and the grace of God or by their own worth to expiate sins and achieve reconciliation with God. They are only eucharistic; by means of them Christians demonstrate their submission and gratitude to God and honor and glorify Him. For since the world has seen only one propitiatory sacrifice, specifically Christ's passion and death, as the Epistle to the Hebrews, chapters 9, 10, 7, etc., most decisively prove (note especially Heb. 10:11, 12, 14), it is clear that all other sacrifices are not propitiatory but are only works whereby believers declare their obedience to God and worship Him. In short, then, these other sacrifices in the New Testament constitute a *thank offering,* that is to say, an act of divine worship, or a good work (a work commanded by God) which we offer to God under the illumination of true faith in Christ, in order that we may honor Him — testify that the One to whom we offer that work is truly God, return thanks by such obedience for benefits we have received, and worship Him; rather than being a payment for sins, or meriting the remission of sins for the offerer or for others, it is an affirmation of our obedience and gratitude to God.

God imparts to us the priestly right, or power, to offer sacrifices

[238] Cf. 1 Cor. 3:16, 17; 6:19, 20.

pleasing to Him, as well as the original source of the true sacrifices of the New Testament, namely, the ministry of the Gospel, or preaching of the divine Word, through which there is kindled in us sound knowledge of God and of our Redeemer Jesus Christ, faith, prayer, love, and conformity with His will. As Paul says in Rom. 15:16: "I am the minister of Jesus Christ, offering the Gospel of God, that the offering up of the Gentiles may be acceptable to God, sanctified[239] by the Holy Ghost"; here the apostle says that he worships and honors God by teaching and preaching the Gospel in order that men may hear and embrace it by faith and thereby become sacrifices pleasing to God, and Holy Spirit-sanctified priests who offer to Him genuine reverence, faith, prayer, and thanksgiving now and throughout eternity. In the course of this present life the true and highest sacrifices of the New Testament are: that we with believing hearts teach, hear, learn, embrace by faith, preach, and confess the Gospel — the true doctrine about God and our Lord Jesus Christ; be converted to God in genuine repentance; fear God; pray, love, and worship Him through trust in Christ the Mediator; endure afflictions patiently and seek and await God's help in them and release from them; thank God and our Lord Jesus Christ for all benefits; rejoice in the Lord; and worship God with a true heart, a reverent voice, and the obedience and conformity of our whole life to His will.

B. *The Spiritual Character of New Testament Thank Offerings*

The cultus of the New Testament is a spiritual one, consisting of genuine conversion to God, faith, and an inner obedience of the heart kindled by the Holy Spirit. There are no other New Testament sacrifices — no external ceremonies of what they call an *opus operatum* rather than *opus operantis* nature,[240] i. e., sacrifices which

[239] Chytraeus, following Codex-Vaticanus, omits the phrase "to the Gentiles," which the AV includes; he supplies an explanatory "to God" after "acceptable"; and he correctly translates the perfect participle ἡγιασμένη by "sanctified" rather than by "being sanctified" (AV). The strongly sacrificial emphasis in this verse is evident from the words λειτουργὸν ("minister"), ἱερουργοῦντα ("ministering/offering/sacrificing"), and προσφορὰ ("offering"). See our author's previous comment on this verse, Section I. B. 2. (3).

[240] *"Opus operatum.* A term used by Roman Catholic theologians with reference to the sacraments to express their doctrine that these sacraments

are pleasing and acceptable to God without true reverence and faith towards Him, that is, without real religion in the heart — and much less does the New Testament set forth sacrifices which merit the remission of sins and eternal life. Indeed, the sacrifices of unbelievers are abominable to the Lord, and those who truly revere God worship Him, not by external actions or ceremonies but in the Spirit and in truth,[241] that is, by real heart activity, true reverence and faith toward God, and inner obedience engendered by the Holy Spirit. The Scriptural testimonies which I shall now cite in order will clearly show what the sacrifices of the New Testament are and of what they consist.

1 Peter 2:5: "Ye are an holy priesthood, to offer up *spiritual sacrifices* acceptable to God by Jesus Christ." These sacrifices are spiritual; they are not the carcasses of animals, such as the Levitical priests offered, or external actions and ceremonies[242] σχήμασι τεχναζόμεναι[243] [artfully contrived with gestures], or even such external works of morality or ethical virtues as Aristides' justice, Pomponius' generosity, or Hippolytus' chastity.[244] By spiritual sacrifices the New Testament means Holy Spirit-motivated attitudes of heart consistent with the will of God — actual conversion to God, real knowledge of Christ, faith, hope, fear of God, love, thanksgiving, and a constant, unwavering will and sincere intention to obey God — and all directed to this end, that He may be honored.

confer the grace of God by the working of the work *(opere operato)*, that is, by the performance of the outward sacramental act, apart from the spiritual condition of the recipient *(opere operantis)*. . . . The Roman doctrine demands only that the recipient do not place an obstacle to grace." *(Lutheran Cyclopedia,* ed. E. L. Lueker [St. Louis: Concordia, 1954], pp. 762, 763; see the entire article.) Cf. note 281.

241 Cf. John 4:23, 24.

242 Here *ceremonia* is misprinted for *ceremoniae.*

243 The accent on this Gk. word has been corrected from penult to antepenult.

244 Aristides' "reputation for honesty went back to his contemporaries, and later became proverbial" (OCD 90). This Athenian statesman and soldier was born ca. 520 B. C. and died ca. 468. Titus Pomponius Atticus (109—32 B. C.) was vastly wealthy and "a discriminating patron of the arts, with a real appreciation of Greek culture, and his house on the Quirinal was a well-known literary centre" (OCD 119). The mythological Hippolytus repulsed the adulterous advances of Phaedra (OCD 431).

This is the first and highest level of sacrifice and, as it were, the soul and life of all other worship and of external sacrificial acts. For without this spiritual obedience of heart, without a true conversion to God, without genuine fear of God, faith in Christ, and the inner obedience which the Holy Spirit produces in harmony with the First Commandment, external worship is nothing, nor do any outward works and sacrifices, however precious or great, please God. For example, the offerings of Cain, of Saul, and of the heathen are not spiritual sacrifices, because their hearts were unbelieving and full of doubts, and thus these offerings escaped God's notice. The prayer and thanksgiving of the Pharisee in Luke 18:9-14 is not a spiritual sacrifice, because his heart was self-confident and irreverent — lacking in real fear of God, trust in the Mediator, and spiritual obedience. And when the heart does not pray, the tongue labors in vain. The acts of generosity on the part of Pomponius Atticus or Cimon [245] do not constitute spiritual sacrifices or a sweet savor unto the Lord,[246] for they were not governed by the Spirit of God or by true knowledge and fear of God and trust in the Mediator, and were not aimed at the worship of God. But the charity of the Philippians [247] and the kindness of the widow of Zarephath toward Elijah [248] are spiritual sacrifices, because they proceeded from God's Spirit — from real fear of God and faith — and were done to proclaim the obedience and gratitude due to God and to render service to a minister of God on God's behalf.

Fear of God and Repentance. Ps. 51:17: "The sacrifices of God are a broken spirit; a broken and a contrite heart, O God, Thou wilt not despise." A heart which truly grieves in repentance and conversion and is in misery,[249] distress, and terror because it knows of its sin and of God's wrath and in faith flees for refuge to the

[245] In Plutarch's biography "Cimon figured as a large-hearted, expansive, genial conservative" (OCD 192). This Athenian soldier and statesman lived ca. 512—449 B. C. For Pomponius Atticus, see the previous note.

[246] Cf. Ex. 29:18; Ezek. 20:41; Eph. 5:2; Phil. 4:18; etc.

[247] To Paul in particular; see Phil. 4:15, 16.

[248] 1 Kings 17:8-24; cf. Luke 4:25, 26.

[249] Lat., *in cruce,* from *crux* ("cross"). Cf. the concept of existential crisis in Kierkegaard.

Mediator, is a most excellent and God-pleasing sacrifice — one with which God is especially satisfied and honored. As Is. 66:2 says: "To what man will I look if not to him that is of a contrite spirit and trembleth at My Word"; also,[250] "God dwelleth with him that is of a contrite and humble spirit, to revive the heart of the contrite ones."

Faith. See Heb. 11:4.

Prayer. Rev. 5:8 states that the prayers of the saints are "thymiamata,"[251] or odors, most pleasing to God. Cf. Ps. 141:2.[252]

Praise and Thanksgiving to God. Read Heb. 13:15;[253] Ps. 116:17; 27:6; 50:14, 15; and note that Ps. 107 declares that a sacrifice of thanksgiving will honor God.[254] To *praise* or *glorify God* is to give Him glory and homage for all His mighty acts and benefits. This means to acknowledge and confess with a true heart, with one's voice, and with full obedience of life that God is indeed wise, omnipotent, holy, truthful, just, merciful, and eternal Father, Son, and Holy Spirit; and that He punishes all the ungodly and receives, hearkens to, and bestows eternal salvation upon every one who in faith flees for refuge to the Son as Mediator. With this knowledge and faith providing illumination, one glorifies God by fearing and loving Him with a true heart, praying to Him, trusting and thanking Him, and obeying Him according to the Word which He has handed down. Thus the praise and glorification of God encompass all the works commanded in the First Table of the Decalog and especially right knowledge of God and the acts of thanking and worshiping Him. A distinguished example of praise to God is furnished by Ambrose and Augustine's canticle, "Te Deum laudamus."[255] To *give thanks* is to acknowledge and

[250] Is. 57:15.

[251] This is a transliteration of the Gk. plural employed in the verse. Souter indicates that θυμίαμα ("incense/perfume") was used in transliteration in Patristic Latin (SGLL 420). Rev. 5:8 (and 8:3, 4) allude to Ps. 141:2.

[252] The erroneous reference to Ps. 131 in the text here has been corrected to Ps. 141 in the translation.

[253] In his rendering of this verse, Chytraeus has "we are offering" instead of the Gk. (and AV) "let us offer."

[254] See especially Ps. 107:22.

[255] "The Te Deum is one of the noblest hymns of the Western Church and one of the greatest confessions of faith in song. . . . A medieval legend,

confess with mind and voice that good things are not bestowed upon us by chance, nor are they merely the product of our own wisdom and industry, but that God actually cares for us, hears us, aids us, and provides us with all our spiritual and material goods.[256] In consequence of this, thanksgiving involves submitting oneself to Him with a true heart and celebrating these divine benefits in plain words, in reverent hymns and praises, and by a life of full obedience — to the end that God may be glorified and many may be encouraged truly to acknowledge and call upon Him.

Benevolence and Charity on the Part of Believers. See Heb. 13:16 and Phil. 4:18.[257]

Righteousness in All Its Aspects. Ps. 4:5: "Offer the sacrifices of righteousness, and put your trust in the Lord." It is therefore a sacrifice of greatest importance to rest on the Lord God with firm faith and trust and under the illumination of real faith in Christ to cultivate righteousness, which means to shun all sin and to obey God in accordance with all His commandments. Thus this precept of the psalmist, "Offer the sacrifices of righteousness," is entirely consistent with Paul's admonition in Rom. 6:12-14, 18, 19 (q. v.). It follows that we may define righteousness as the total obedience which is owed to the Law, that is, conformity of mind, will, heart — of all one's plans, words, and outward actions — to the eternal and steadfast norm of uprightness, the will of God. Righteousness then embraces all virtues and all the duties we owe to

current since the eighth century, credited its joint authorship to Ambrose and Augustine upon the occasion of the baptism of the latter by the former. Modern scholars generally accept the suggestion, first advanced by Dom Morin in 1894, that Niceta, missionary bishop of Remesiana in Dacia (A. D. 335—414), was the author or at least the compiler of the Hymn." (Luther D. Reed, *The Lutheran Liturgy* [Philadelphia: Muhlenberg Press, 1947], pp. 392, 393)

[256] Chytraeus' use here of both the accusative-and-infinitive and a *quod* clause after the same verbs introducing indirect discourse is certainly not a classical device; it does, however, have excellent Patristic precedent. Cf. the following sentence from Augustine's account of his conversion: "Audieram enim de Antonio, quod ex evangelica lectione, cui forte supervenerat, admonitus fuerit, tamquam sibi diceretur quod legebatur: vade, vende omnia, quae habes, da pauperibus et habebis thesaurum in caelis; et veni, sequere me, et tali oraculo confestim ad te esse conversum" (*Confessions* VIII, xii, 29).

[257] In quoting this verse the text incorrectly has *nostra* for *vostra (vestra).*

God and to our fellowmen. It is indeed true that ἐν δὲ δικαιοσύνῃ συλλήβδην πᾶσ' ἀρετή ἐστιν (righteousness contains all virtues in herself).[258]

Complete New Obedience Toward God in Accord with All His Commands. Rom. 12:1,2: "Now[259] I beseech you, brethren, by the mercies of God, that ye present" (or bring) "your bodies a living sacrifice, holy, acceptable unto God, which is your reasonable service. And be not conformed to this world; but be ye transformed by the renewing of your mind that ye may prove what is that good and acceptable and perfect will of God." This remarkable entreaty of Paul shows very clearly what constitutes the New Testament sacrifices and worship that are to be offered to God by all Christians alike — by all whom the Spirit of Christ has consecrated and anointed priests through Baptism. Specifically, we believers are to present, not the bodies of animals or other substances devoid not only of reason but also of consciousness but our very own minds, wills, hearts, ideas, plans, desires, and our every outward action — and these in a Holy Spirit-renovated condition; and our virtues as well as all the sins which displease God are to be obediently presented to Him, i. e., conformed to the good and perfect will of God revealed to us through the commands in His Word. Just as in the case of the Levitical sacrifices there was a command to offer bodies (the bodies of animals sacrificed to God at the door of the tabernacle), so Paul orders all Christians — the priests of the New Covenant — to offer bodies. But these are not the bodies of lambs or bulls, nor are they loaves, cakes, or other inanimate things, but their very own bodies. And this means them-

---

258 Theognis of Megara (6th century B.C.), quoted by Phocylides (Fragment 15). "Next to Solon, the greatest [Classical Greek] exponent of the idea of justice is Theognis, among whose sayings the famous verse occurs: 'In justice all virtue is comprehended.' Justice is here, in this early period, not an inner quality, but the legally prescribed behavior of the citizen toward society. This explains how all virtues came to be included in the later conception of δικαιοσύνη." (Hermann Kleinknecht, in Gottfried Quell and Gottlob Schrenk, *Righteousness,* trans. from Gerhard Kittel's *Theologisches Wörterbuch zum Neuen Testament,* and ed. with additions, by J. R. Coates [London: A. & C. Black, 1951], p. 10)

259 The οὖν in the Gk. of this verse is better translated "therefore" *(itaque)* than "now" *(autem),* as the larger context of the passage indicates. See William Sanday and A. C. Headlam, *Romans* (ICC), 5th ed. (Edinburgh: T. & T. Clark, 1902), pp. 351, 352.

selves, for Paul συνεκδοχικῶς [by way of synecdoche] [260] here comprehends the whole man under only his physical nature, as in the next chapter, Rom. 13:1, he employs another aspect of man's being in a similar way: "Let every soul be subject unto powers." [261] Christians should offer God their minds, wills, plans, endeavors, desires, and their entire life activity as a sacrifice to Him; and they should dedicate them to God's use — to activities which please Him and serve His glory — as 1 Cor. 10:31 says, "Do all to the glory of God." Believers must, as Paul says, immolate and destroy — or mortify — not various kinds of living creatures but their wicked ideas; doubts; lusts; depraved desires; carnal security; pride; self-esteem; inordinate love of pleasure, money, and glory; the passions of hatred, sensuality, envy, wrath, and revenge; etc. They are to begin a new, holy, and God-pleasing life, involving clear, sound knowledge of God, living faith and trust in Him, and pure, holy obedience toward all His commands. In this way they will offer or present themselves to God "a holy sacrifice," i. e., pure, clean, consecrated to Him; as well as "a living sacrifice," i. e., freed from sin and death and vivified with new righteousness through the Son of God, who is the Λόγος [Word], [262] the Source and Giver of eternal life, and the Sacrifice who is forever with God the Father.

Indeed, the just and living God has created men, has redeemed them through His Son, and sanctifies them by His Spirit in order that He may communicate Himself and the highest and best that He has — life, light, wisdom, and righteousness — to them, and that they in turn may be conformed to Him through possession of similar life, light, wisdom, and righteousness and may celebrate His goodness with reverent minds, thankful voices, and total obedience

---

[260] This adverb appears in Diodorus Siculus (5.31) but is probably a gloss. See L-S II, 1706.

[261] This sentence shows quite clearly that Chytraeus understood the monistic character of Pauline psychology. He thus agrees with Luther that a dualism cannot be created between "soul/spirit" on the one hand, and "body/flesh" on the other, with the former considered "good" and the latter "evil." To Paul, Luther, and our author the axioms "totus homo caro" and "totus homo spiritus" must both be applied to the believer, and Christian responsibility in every realm involves the entire human being — body and soul. See Eino Sormunen, *Jumalan Armo* (Helsinki, 1934), especially Vol. II, pp. 112, 113, 304, 305.

[262] John 1:1-18.

of life. This Paul declares in Rom. 12:1, 2 by immediately indicating what he means by "a living and holy sacrifice": Be not conformed to this evil world, but let there dawn in you a new spiritual light, a new righteousness, a life in harmony with God's good and perfect will and acceptable to Him on account of His beloved Son. This constitutes a "reasonable service," for the mind, having been renewed by the Holy Spirit, knows God's beneficent will as it is revealed in Law and Gospel, and, under the illumination provided by true knowledge of the Mediator and trust in Him, obeys God in accord with His every command and to the end that He may be glorified. This is not the case with pagan worship, in which, though worthwhile external acts are performed, the mind is ignorant of the true God, without knowledge of the Mediator, and does not aim at the glorification of God in what it does. The sacrifices and worship services of Pharisees are likewise irrational and ἄλογοι [unreasonable], for the worshiper's heart feels no genuine fear of God, repentance, or faith in Christ and supposes that it makes itself acceptable to God *ex opere operato*.[263] So Paul repeats and explains what he calls λογικὴ λατρεία, or "reasonable service," by giving the command μὴ συσχηματίζεσθε, "be not conformed." [264] He means that we should not become shaped by or similar to the world, or ungodly men, through maintaining their wicked [gg] beliefs

263 See above, note 240.

264 Phillips gives the following magnificent rendering of Rom. 12:1, 2: "With eyes wide open to the mercies of God, I beg you, my brothers, as an act of intelligent worship, to give Him your bodies, as a living sacrifice, consecrated to Him and acceptable by Him. Don't let the world around you squeeze you into its own mould, but let God re-mould your minds from within, so that you may prove in practice that the Plan of God for you is good, meets all His demands and moves towards the goal of true maturity." (J. B. Phillips, *Letters to Young Churches* [New York: Macmillan, 1947], p. 27). The use of the present imperative rather than the aorist subjunctive in the prohibition "be not conformed" indicates that Paul wished the Romans to stop a conforming already in process — that he was not writing to warn them against a conformity of which they were only in danger (see James Hope Moulton, *A Grammar of New Testament Greek*, I, 3d ed. [Edinburgh: T. & T. Clark, 1908], 122—126). These verses, together with Chytraeus' valuable exposition of them, should be of more than passing interest to Christians of our day — a day when conformity to God seems to pale before conformity of the grey-flannel-suit, organization-man, other-directed variety (cf. W. H. Whyte, Jr., *The Organization Man;* David Riesman, *The Lonely Crowd*).

about God and carnal affections such as complacency, suspicion, pride, selfish ambition, hatred, envy, avarice, and inordinate love of pleasure and glory and distinction. "But [hh] be ye transformed by the renewing of your mind that ye may prove what is that good and perfect will of God," that is, let your minds be conformed to God's will and renewed through the Holy Spirit. Transformed minds are characterized by a new and clear knowledge of the will of God and of our Lord Jesus Christ as that will is revealed in His Word; by a genuine fear of God and faith in Him; and by a new righteousness involving obedience and conformity to the God in whose image they were made in the beginning. Paul presents this same thought in almost the same words in Eph. 4:22-24.

Malachi also speaks of these sacrifices of the New Covenant which are carried out among us through the ministry, or preaching of the Gospel. In 1:11 we read: "From the rising of the sun even unto the going down of the same My name shall be great" (or glorified) "among the Gentiles." Here Malachi prophesies that God and His benefits will be rightly known and proclaimed (God now shows us these benefits in Christ) and that everywhere the incense of believing prayer will be offered to God, together with that sacrifice of unalloyed thanksgiving and of obedience toward God which proceeds from a heart that is pure and cleansed through faith in Christ. Concerning this purification, Malachi says a little later (in 3:3) that Christ [265] "shall purify the sons of Levi, and they shall offer unto the Lord an offering in righteousness."

All of the above Scriptural testimonies illustrate the definition of New Testament sacrifices previously set forth, and clearly indicate what these sacrifices are and what characterizes them. In particular, the Bible has shown that they are spiritual acts of worship — true heart actions — virtues kindled by the Holy Spirit, and these include genuine fear of God, real faith (i. e., knowledge of and trust in Christ as Mediator), prayer and praise to God, and a hearty obedience which is in conformity with His will. Moreover, we have seen that such transformation of heart must light the way for all other forms of worship, that is to say, for ceremonies and external moral actions.

[265] The punctuation of the Latin sentence has been altered slightly at this point in the interest of grammar and contextual meaning.

C. *A Word from Prudentius and an Application of the Decalog*

Prudentius, in his "Crown of Romanus the Martyr," has expressed this doctrine of Christian priesthood and sacrifice in illustrious, distinguished words and unsurpassed verses. I therefore encourage young readers to become thoroughly conversant with the following lines:

> You have heard what He is; learn now the way and manner of worshipping Him, the nature of His temple, the gifts He has ordained to be dedicated to Him, the prayers He calls for, the priests He would have, the sweet savour He commands to be sacrificed to Him there. A temple He has established for Himself in the soul of man, one that is living, clear, perceptive, spiritual, incapable of dissolution or destruction, beautiful, graceful, high-topped, coloured with different hues. There stands the priestess in the sacred doorway; the virgin Faith guards the first entrance, her hair bound with queenly ties, and calls for sacrifices to be offered to Christ and the Father which are pure and sincere, such as she knows are acceptable to them — a modest bearing, an innocent heart, unruffled peace, chastity of body, the fear of God which is the measure of knowledge, sober abstinence in fastings, hope ever erect, a hand ever generous. From these offerings arises a pleasing steam which surpasses the scent of balsam or incense or saffron or air drenched in eastern perfumes. It mounts from them and is carried right to heaven, where it wins favour with God and gives Him sweet delight. Whosoever is an enemy to this teaching and forbids it, forbids the good life and the pursuit of holiness, forbids us to direct the soul's activity on high; etc.[266]

[266] Chytraeus quotes Prudentius' *Peristephanon liber* ("Crowns of Martyrdom"), x. 341—368. In a seventh-century manuscript, Hymn Ten is titled, "The Declarations of St. Romanus the Martyr against the Pagans" (Romanus was a deacon at Caesarea who suffered at Antioch in 303); it seems probable that this Hymn was originally a separate publication. I have employed Thomson's prose translation: *Prudentius,* with an English tr. by H. J. Thomson, II (Cambridge: Harvard University Press [Loeb Classical Library], 1953), 252—255. Aurelius Clemens Prudentius (348—ca. 410), who has been called "the Horace and Vergil of the Christians," was among the most widely read authors during the middle ages; his *Peristephanon liber* greatly influenced the iconography of medieval art.

A^{ll} most satisfactory enumeration of spiritual sacrifices can be made on the basis of the precepts of the Decalog as interpreted by the Gospel. In this way, all forms of worship — the sacrifices owed to God, i. e., all the good works which He requires of us — appear in very systematic arrangement. Thus we have: [267] [1] True knowledge and worship of the Lord God and our Redeemer Jesus Christ; real fear of God (meaning contrition and repentance); genuine faith and confidence which rests in the Lord; and joyful obedience to all His commands — obedience issuing forth from an ardent love of Him. [2] True prayer to God; hope of divine aid and His liberating power; patience in troubles and afflictions; preaching and confessing the truth about God; and praising and thanking Him. [3] Expounding and hearing the doctrine of God as it is proclaimed in the public ministry; the studies of those who teach and learn in schools; reverence and obedience toward the clergy; and contributions or offerings for the support of the ministry. [4] Justice in all matters, that is, with real fear of God and faith in Christ providing the illumination, obedience to all just laws, magistrates, parents, and teachers; and the diligent, assiduous performance — to the glory of God — of the duties belonging to one's vocation, whether political, domestic, ecclesiastical, or educational.[268] [5] Not harming by force or fraud another's life, body, reputation, or possessions, but for the Lord's sake doing good to others through counsel, instruction, work, and money, and rendering to everyone the duties and honor owed him; on the basis of genuine fear and love of God and one's neighbor, exercising toward others gentleness, placability, ἐπιείκεια [graciousness],[269]

[267] With this enumeration of Christian sacrifices on the basis of the Ten Commandments, cf. Part One of Luther's Small and Large Catechisms. The use of the Decalog as a scheme of organization in theological discussion is well illustrated by Melanchthon's chapter on natural law in the later (revised and expanded) editions of his *Loci communes*.

[268] The great contribution of Lutheran theology in the matter of *Beruf* or *vocatio* should be noted in this connection; see especially Gustaf Wingren, *Luther on Vocation*, trans. C. C. Rasmussen (Philadelphia: Muhlenberg Press, 1957); Einar Billing, *Our Calling*, trans. Conrad Bergendoff (Rock Island, Ill.: Augustana Book Concern, 1947); and Edgar M. Carlson, "Stewardship and Christian Vocation," in T. K. Thompson, ed., *Stewardship in Contemporary Theology* (New York: Association Press, 1960), pp. 183 to 203.

[269] Chytraeus was wise not to attempt to translate this word. "No Latin

mercy, clemency, sincerity, fidelity, kindness, and whatever else human beings owe their fellows; by the just use of arms, bravely defending one's country, the church, school, one's family, public order, etc.;[270] and encouraging peace and harmony among all. [6] Reverently upholding the virtues of chastity and decency whether one is married or single; and living soberly unto prayer.[271] [7] Preserving justice and equity in contractual obligations. [8] Being truthful in theology, in science and art, in senate chamber and courtroom (whether one serves as judge, witness, plaintiff, or defendant), in remarks about the virtues and vices of others — in short, in every word and deed throughout one's life; thinking and speaking of oneself in modest and accurate terms; listening to and heeding sound warnings and advice from others; and keeping control over one's mind and tongue, so that the things one says may be acceptable to God and beneficial to man. [9-10] Lastly, curbing and mortifying (as Paul says) all wicked affections and desires — inordinate love of pleasure and money and glory and power, pride, selfish ambition, irascibility, hatred, envy, vindictiveness, carnal security indifferent to the wrath and judgment of God, murmuring and indignation against God when faced with hardships, etc.; and possessing new affections — new attitudes of heart and will — in conformity with God's will and aimed especially at our glorifying Him.

D. *The Christian Thank Offering in Its Proper Perspective*

Now [31] these sacrifices cannot be offered to God by human strength alone or by the power of man's free will. It is God

word exactly and adequately renders it; 'clementia' sets forth one side of it, 'aequitas' another, and perhaps 'modestia' (by which the Vulgate translates it, 2 Cor. x. 1) a third; but the word is wanting which should set forth all these excellencies reconciled in a single and a higher one" (R. C. Trench, *Synonyms of the New Testament,* 9th ed. [Grand Rapids: Eerdmans, 1948 (reprinting the London 1880 issue)], p. 154, n. 1; see this splendid discussion *in toto,* pp. 153—157).

270 Historic Lutheran theology has never been hospitable to the pacifistic position. See in this connection L. J. Roehm, "The Christian's Attitude Towards His Government and on War," *Concordia Theological Monthly,* XII (May 1941), 321—339.

271 Lat., *sobrium esse ad precationem.* Our author seems to be thinking principally of 1 Peter 4:7, but he may also have 1 Cor. 7:5 in mind, since *sobrius* can mean "continent."

Himself who, through our hearing, reading, and reflecting upon His Word, that is, the Gospel, illumines our minds with real knowledge of Christ the Mediator and trust in Him, vivifies our wills and hearts, which have been freed from sin and death by His Son, and pours out upon them the Spirit of grace and prayer. The Spirit's task is to kindle in us, for the glory of God, a new righteousness (meaning conformity with His will), an ardent and genuine love of the Lord, a joyful obedience of the heart to Him, and the performance — not out of fear of punishment but from a love of God and neighbor — of the deeds which He commands. This is made clear by the following Scriptural verses: 1 Peter 1:23; 2:4-6;[272] Heb. 13:15; Mal. 3:3; John 15:5 ("Without Me" — Christ — "ye can do nothing," i. e., nothing acceptable to God or beneficial to yourselves or others); Gal. 5:22.

Christian[kk] thank offerings do not please God *ex opere operato*[273] — on account of their inherent worth. For even in the case of all the believers and saints, many sins remain, such as ignorance about God and numerous evil inclinations and residual affections, and these prevent our obedience from satisfying the Law or commending itself to God because of its intrinsic excellence. Paul teaches us this at some length in Rom. 7; verse 23 reads:[274] "I see another law" (the dominion and power of sin) "in my members" (in my faculties of soul and body), "warring against the law of my mind" (my mind illumined by the Holy Spirit), "and bringing me into captivity to sin." Note also Ps. 32:5,6, and 1 John 1:10—2:2. It follows, then, that our sacrifices of praise are accepted by God, not because of their inherent worthiness but because of the mediation of Jesus Christ His Son, through faith in Him (see 1 Peter 2:5).

For, in the first place, it is necessary that a priest — a person who offers sacrifice — be one who is acceptable and pleasing to God, that is to say, one who has been reconciled freely, for the

272 Only 1 Peter 2 is cited, though the quotation given in the text begins with 1 Peter 1:23.

273 See above, note 240.

274 Chytraeus thus agrees with Augustine, the Latin fathers generally, and Luther in applying this Romans 7 passage to the regenerate rather than to the unregenerate man. The opposing position is represented by Origen and the majority of Greek fathers.

sake of God's Son, by faith, without which it is impossible to please God or come to Him.[275] This is shown by Gen. 4:4;[276] Prov. 15:8; Ps. 147:11 ("The Lord taketh pleasure in them that fear Him, in those that hope in His mercy," viz., in the mercy promised by reason of Christ the Mediator); and Rom. 3:24, 25. Second, the priest — this person who for the sake of Christ has been reconciled[277] and is pleasing to God — should recognize and deplore the multiplicity of sins still clinging to us, among which are our ignorance and doubts concerning God; our carnal security; the feebleness and listlessness of our faith, prayer, hope, love, and the other virtues; impatience and consternation when faced with hardships; pride and self-conceit in favorable circumstances; and inordinate passions of lust, hatred, and desire for revenge. As a holy priest he should beseech God to pardon him and remit these sins for the sake of Christ the Mediator, who intercedes in our behalf, for Christ teaches us to pray, "Forgive us our trespasses"; and at the same time he should endeavor by the Spirit to mortify his sins and amend his life.[278] Third, even in the face of what has just been said, the Christian priest should hold the conviction that it is God's eternal and unchangeable will that we offer to Him the sacrifices commanded in His Word, that is, present Him with good works and the worship which is acceptable to Him; and he should firmly believe that such acts of worship, on the part of us who have been reborn through His Word and built in faith on Christ, the living Rock,[279] do please God and are accepted by Him because of Christ, our Propitiator, who is now interceding for us.

Under[11] no condition ought we to offer God sacrifices of praise in order to merit the remission of sins or righteousness and eternal life by so doing; for these benefits have been freely provided and given to us through that sacrifice of our Lord Jesus Christ, the only Son of God, which was accomplished once for all on the cross in our behalf. The proper reasons for presenting

[275] Heb. 11:6.

[276] As interpreted by Heb. 11:4.

[277] *Reconliata* is misprinted for *reconciliata* in the text here.

[278] Note that the Scriptural paradox of human responsibility and divine activity in sanctification, as set forth especially in Phil. 2:12, 13, is given effective expression here.

[279] 1 Peter 1:23, 2:4-6.

Christian thank offerings are to show, by every kind of obedient act and demonstration of praise to God, the gratitude which we owe Him for His benefits; to obey reverently those unqualified commands of God (we reminded the reader of them a little way back) which require us to offer the sacrifices enjoined by Him; and to honor God by testifying that we really believe and profess that the One to whom we present rightful obedience and worship is the only true God, and by introducing other men to true knowledge and worship of Him through our example. To these licit and principal ends can also be added the other, lesser purposes: escape from the punishments connected with unbelief and neglect of the sacrifices or obedience owed to God, and attainment of the spiritual and material rewards in this life and throughout eternity which have been promised to those who obey God — that is, to believing priests.[280]

[280] Though they are unquestionably of "lesser" importance, as Chytraeus says, these reasons for Christian sacrificial conduct are still legitimate, for they have solid Scriptural warrant. The fear of God is a motivation appealed to in both Testaments (not just the Old), and the New Testament has much to say on the matter of "rewards" (see, e. g., Matt. 10:42; Eph. 6:8; Rev. 22:12). The danger in such appeals to fear or reward lies, of course, in the ease with which they can be misunderstood and interpreted in unevangelical ways.

VI

THE SACRIFICE OF THE MASS

A. *The Lines Are Drawn*

We have recounted in detail above, and refuted at length,[mm] the general errors which contradict a sound doctrine of sacrifice. It is not unreasonable that we should now add certain remarks with regard to the outstanding perversion of the New Testament's teaching on priesthood and sacrifice.

Not only do the adherents of the pope arrogate the honor and right of priesthood — which is equally common to all Christians — solely to those priests who have been consecrated and tonsured in papist fashion, but by their impious and idolatrous sacrifice of the Mass they corrupt the entire New Testament doctrine of priesthood and sacrifice. For they suppose that an external, visible priesthood and sacrifice must at all times exist in the church of the New Covenant and that in the Christian church this sacrifice is the Mass. They maintain that in the sacrifice of the Mass the priest offers to God the body and blood of our Lord Jesus Christ and sets God's Son in the presence of His eternal Father. And they declare that this oblation of Christ's body and blood is the chief act of worship and the continual sacrifice of the church of the New Testament, and that by offering it for others, living or dead, one may apply to them the fruits and benefits of Christ's sacrifice on the cross.[281]

[281] This is a fair and accurate statement of the Roman position as solidified in the pronouncements of the Council of Trent (1545—63), which took place only a few years before the publication of Chytraeus' *De sacrificiis* (1569). Cf. the following Tridentine definitions: "Una eademque est hostia, idem nunc offerens sacerdotum ministerio, qui se ipsum tunc in cruce obtulit, sola offerendi ratione diversa"; "Si quis dixerit, Missae sacrificium tantum esse laudis et gratiarum actionis . . . non autem propitiatorium . . . neque pro vivis et defunctis, pro peccatis, poenis, satisfactionibus et aliis necessitatibus offerri debere, A. S." It should be noted, however, that in recent years a number of Roman Catholic scholars (especially in Europe) have attempted to reinterpret the Sacrament in personalistic terms (see the writings of the Dutch Roman Catholic H. Schillebeeckx; the Jesuit Francis Clark's *Eucharistic Sacrifice and the Reformation;* B. Leeming's *Principles of*

The Standard of Truth in the Argument over the Sacrifice of the Mass. Now, although we agree that this doctrine is the basic foundation and strength of papal religion and rule, and although there are very many who think that to shatter or overthrow it is not only rebellious but also wicked and blasphemous, nevertheless one does well to prefer God's glory and heavenly truth to the might and influence of the wise and powerful. And in this whole argument there is a single absolute and unalterable norm of truth: the express word of our Lord Jesus Christ, the Son of God, who in instituting and establishing His testament — the Lord's Supper — which they call the Mass, "on the night in which He was betrayed, took bread; and when He had given thanks, He brake it and gave it to His disciples, saying, Take, eat; this is My body, which is broken for you; this do in remembrance of Me. After the same manner also He took the cup when He had supped, saying, Drink ye all of it; this is the cup of the new testament in My blood, which is given and shed for you for the remission of sins. This do ye, as oft as ye drink it, in remembrance of Me. For as often as ye eat this bread and drink this cup, ye do show the Lord's death till He come." [282] Both in their private deliberations on this question and in their arguments with opponents, students should direct their eyes and their hearts to these words with which the Supper was instituted and which have come down to us from Christ; they should lean upon them, and they should not allow themselves to be turned aside or led away from them by any πιθανολογία [persuasive argumentation].[283] For in matters of religion one must follow, not the customs and precepts of the pope or of any other human being, but the truth of the only God.

Sacramental Theology; Louis Bouyer's *Liturgical Piety;* and cf. Protestant Ernest B. Koenker's *The Liturgical Renaissance in the Roman Catholic Church);* these herculean efforts are laudable from a Biblical standpoint, but the basic question is whether the Tridentine formulations do not in the final analysis militate against such reinterpretations of the Mass.

[282] The last sentence is not part of the Verba but immediately follows them in 1 Cor. 11:26. The *Apostolic Constitutions* viii, 12, 16, puts these words of Paul into Christ's mouth. See Archibald Robertson and Alfred Plummer, *The First Epistle of St. Paul to the Corinthians* (ICC), 2d ed. (Edinburgh: T. & T. Clark, 1914), p. 249.

[283] Plato employs this word to refer to the use of arguments based on probability, as contrasted with ἀπόδειξις (demonstration).

I have set forth all the various aspects of the doctrine of the Lord's Supper, together with a short refutation of the errors embodied in the papist Mass, in my recent exposition of the words [nn] of institution as transmitted by Matthew in chap. 26 of his Gospel.[284] The studious should therefore supplement the present discussion by means of it — or rather, with pertinent material from those richer treatises of Luther: *On the Abrogation of Private Mass* and *The Babylonian Captivity*.[285]

[oo] The Mass, or Lord's Supper, is Christ's testament, that is,

[284] Chytraeus directs the reader's attention to his *Commentary on Matthew*, which was published in at least two editions and several printings during his lifetime. Since the dedicatory epistle to the first edition is dated March 25, 1555, we have a definite *terminus ad quem* for the composition of the work. But since the *Commentary* originated in Chytraeus' university lectures and was seen through the press by another (Samuel Isenmenger, who wrote the dedicatory epistle), one cannot determine from this a precise date of composition. Concordia Seminary (St. Louis, Mo.) has in its library a 1558 printing of this edition (*Commentarius in Matthaeum evangelistam, ex praelectionibus Davidis Chytraei collectus* [Wittenberg: J. Crato, 1558], 581 pp.). The *Catalogue général des livres imprimés* of the Bibliothèque Nationale in Paris lists a 1560 printing likewise brought out by Crato. Chytraeus' biographer O. F. Schütz used a 1566 printing of the work (see his *De vita Davidis Chytraei*, I [Hamburg: Fickweiler, 1720], 123). The University of Chicago Library's Special Collections contains a copy of the second edition, titled: *In Matthaeum evangelistam enarratio, ex praelectionibus Davidis Chytraei. Recens recognita. Accesserunt huic editioni prolegomena utilia . . .* (Wittenberg?, 1575), 757 pp.; all prefatory matter is dropped from this edition, and the "prolegomena" are added. The importance of the *Commentary on Matthew* to the *De sacrificiis* lies in the fact that from this point to the last sentence of the work the *De sacrificiis*, Chytraeus takes his material almost verbatim from the *Commentary on Matthew*, chap. 26, where one finds a detailed discussion "de Coena Domini." In the 1575 ed. the material taken over into the *De sacrificiis* covers pp. 640—644, 646—654 (the entire "Lord's Supper" essay appearing on pp. 612—654).

[285] In the present work Chytraeus has been much influenced by these all-important pamphlets from the pen of his former teacher. On Luther's conception of the Lord's Supper, see especially the following recent publications: Hermann Sasse, *This Is My Body* (Minneapolis: Augsburg, 1959); Vilmos Vajta, *Luther on Worship*, trans. U. S. Leupold (Philadelphia: Muhlenberg Press, 1958); Jaroslav Pelikan, *Luther the Expositor: Introduction to the Reformer's Exegetical Writings*, companion volume to *Luther's Works: American Edition* (St. Louis: Concordia, 1959), Part II: "The Practice of Luther's Exegesis: A Case Study," dealing with Luther's exegesis of several key Eucharistic texts; and Helmut T. Lehmann, ed., *Meaning and Practice of the Lord's Supper* (Philadelphia: Muhlenberg Press, 1961), chap. iv.

a promise of the remission of sins which was sealed by Christ's death; it is at the same time the distribution and partaking of His body and blood. That it is not a sacrifice in which we offer Christ's body and blood to God is plainly demonstrated by the words of institution, where almost every letter [286] contradicts the fundamental idea of such a sacrifice. Christ broke the bread and gave it to His disciples, saying: "Take . . ."; but to receive something from another is not to offer and sacrifice it to the one who is giving. In the Supper we are commanded by God to receive the body and blood of Christ and the remission of our sins; consequently, we are not supposed to offer these same things to God. Moreover, it is clearer than the noonday sun that the words "eat, drink" are diametrically opposed particularly to the concept [287] of the whole burnt offering, all of which was sacrificed to God and none of which was allowed to be eaten — even by the priests. Then Christ says: "This is My body, which is given for you. This is My blood, which is shed for you for the remission of sins." It is evident that these words are words of promise by which God offers and imparts His benefits to us, and [288] that they are at the same time seals or pledges of His promise. Now a promise (by which God confers His benefits upon us) is utterly in conflict with a sacrifice (in which we ourselves offer something of our own to God); and seals or pledges are not customarily given to a promiser, whereas a promiser does receive and retain sacrificial offerings. From these Verba handed down by Christ we conclude most unmistakably that in the Mass, or Lord's Supper, Christ's body and blood are not offered to God either as a propitiatory or as a eucharistic sacrifice [289] but are given and presented by God through a minister and are only taken and received by us.

[286] Quintilian used the word *apex* for the long mark over a vowel, and the diminutive *apiculus* was employed ca. 1515 to refer to a Gk. breathing mark. *Apex* = "a letter of the alphabet" was an established ecclesiastical Lat. usage. (See particularly B-J 22)

[287] *Natura* must be supplied in the text at this point; the construction exactly parallels that in the second English (the first Latin) sentence of this same paragraph.

[288] *Et* is required here.

[289] Because of their anthropocentric, Romanist associations, Chytraeus prefers not to apply either the adjective "sacrificial" or the term "eucharistic" to the Lord's Supper. As we have seen above (note 236), he uses the ex-

Therefore the celebration of the Lord's Supper, consisting of the distribution and partaking of the body and blood of Christ, cannot properly be called a propitiatory or a eucharistic sacrifice when considered by itself and apart from the faith, prayer, thanksgiving, etc., of those partaking. Christ, in fact, nowhere refers to it as a sacrifice but calls it a testament, that is, the promise of One about to die who is distributing His goods to His heirs. And since no one should alter a man's will either by adding to or detracting from it (Gal. 3:15), how much less ought men to have turned into a sacrifice the Supper of the Lord — the personal testament of our Lord Jesus Christ, the Son of God — in which not a single mention of sacrifice or oblation is made.

The following solid and impregnable argument will show that the Mass, defined in the papistic manner as a priestly sacrifice, does not merit the remission of sins for the one saying it or for others, and thus is not a propitiatory sacrifice: The one sacrifice of Christ, in which He offered Himself once for all on the cross to the eternal Father, merits the remission of sins and eternal salvation for all who apply that sacrifice to themselves by faith and by the use of the Sacrament (Heb. 9:26; 10:14).[290] Now it is evident that the Mass is not this one sacrifice of Christ which was made once for all on the altar of the cross. Ergo, the Mass does not merit the remission of sins for the priest who says it or for others.[291]

pression "eucharistic sacrifices" to refer to general Christian thank offerings. In harmony with Article XXIV of the Apology of the Augsburg Confession, modern Lutheran liturgical scholars and theologians, having the benefit of greater historical perspective, do not object to the use of these well-established terms, provided they are defined in a sound, evangelical way. See Yngve Brilioth, *Eucharistic Faith & Practice, Evangelical & Catholic*, trans. A. G. Hebert (London: S. P. C. K., 1930); and Gustaf Aulén, *Eucharist and Sacrifice*, trans. E. H. Wahlstrom (Philadelphia: Muhlenberg Press, 1958). Cf. the text at note 19.

290 With Chytraeus' frequent quotation of and allusion to Heb. 9:26, cf. Jaroslav Pelikan's discussion of the place of this verse in Luther's thinking, *Luther the Expositor* [see note 285], pp. 237—254.

291 The force of this reasoning is well recognized in Roman circles; the following is a typical attempt to avoid the horns of the dilemma: "While the Sacrifice on the Cross is an absolute sacrifice, as it is neither the commemoration of a past sacrifice nor the archtype of a future sacrifice, the Sacrifice of the Mass is a relative sacrifice, as it is essentially linked to the Sacrifice on the Cross. . . . It follows from the relativity of the Sacrifice of

Further, since the remission of sins is given *freely* because of Christ alone and not by virtue of any work on our part, and since we receive it by faith alone, as every statement in the Gospel testifies, it is absolutely incorrect that the work of a priest saying Mass earns the remission of sins.

Utterly false, too, is their supposition that the Lord's Supper, or the Mass, can be applied to others. For no sacraments, insofar as they are sacraments, can be applied to those who do not themselves use them; for example, no one can receive absolution for another [292] or be baptized for another. The rite of Baptism does a person no good if he himself is not baptized! Christ's sacrifice is applied, not by reason of the work of someone else — a priest — but by virtue of each person's own faith and use of the sacrament, as John 17:19, 20 indicates.

And it is a ghastly mistake for them to apply the Lord's Supper to the dead and to think that the sacrifice of the Mass frees the souls of the dead from purgatory. This error is clearly refuted by the three arguments to follow: First, the Lord's Supper profits only those who partake of it and who remember Christ's benefits, as the words "Take," "Eat," "Drink," "Do this in remembrance of Me" unequivocally show. But the dead do not themselves partake of the Lord's Supper; they do not receive, eat, and drink the body and blood of Christ. Therefore, the papist Masses do not

the Mass that it in no way detracts from the Sacrifice of the Cross [!]" (Ludwig Ott, *Fundamentals of Catholic Dogma,* ed. J. C. Bastible, trans. Patrick Lynch [St. Louis: Herder, 1958 (*nihil obstat, imprimatur,* 1954)], p. 407).

[292] "Luther rejected the sacrament of Penance, but retained the 'Power of the Keys,' the authority of the Pastoral office to declare and pronounce unto all men being penitent the absolution and remission of their sins. It is for him an essential part of the Ministry of the Word. Cf. *W. A.* XLII. 636. 32 ff.: 'We have several visible tokens: first, Baptism itself, adorned with a most sweet and solemn promise, that if we believe, we shall be saved. But since in this weakness of ours we easily slip, there are added to Baptism the Keys, or the Ministry of the Word (for these are not to be separated), which itself also is a visible token of grace, bound up with the voice of the Gospel according to Christ's institution: "What things soever ye shall loose on earth shall be loosed in heaven." When thou apprehendest this word by faith, thou art restored again to grace.'" (Philip S. Watson, *Let God Be God! An Interpretation of the Theology of Martin Luther* [London: Epworth Press, 1947], p. 183, n. 105)

do the dead a bit of good. Second, "Blessed are the dead which die in the Lord";[293] "Today shalt thou be with Me in paradise" (Luke 23:43); and "He that believeth not shall be condemned." [294] These verses prove that when they depart this life, believers enter into true blessedness, but unbelievers are condemned. There is, consequently, no halfway house — no purgatory — where souls after death may make satisfaction for their sins; and Masses for souls in purgatory are artificial, useless, and idolatrous. Lastly, we read in 2 Cor. 5:10: "We must all appear before the judgment seat of Christ, that everyone may receive the things done in his body . . ."; thus there is no opportunity for repentance after death.

B. *The Fallacious Arguments of Rome*

There are three principal arguments which the papists employ when they try to defend in a somewhat plausible vein that horrible profanation of the Lord's Supper which occurs in the sacrifice of the Mass.

The First Argument. "Christ says in the Verba of the Lord's Supper, 'This do in remembrance of Me.' Therefore, in the Supper a priest ought not merely to distribute the body and blood of Christ but also to make a commemorative sacrifice in which Christ is offered to God, and the fruit of Christ's sacrifice is applied to others."

I answer this argument by denying the conclusion, and my reason is that many things are woven into the conclusion which cannot be deduced from the premise. For it is plain that in the words of the Lord's Supper no mention at all is made of sacrifice, oblation, or application. Rather, Christ offers and presents His own body and blood to us and commands us to take, eat, drink, and do this in commemoration, or remembrance, of Him, i. e., to do it because He gave His body for us and shed His blood for the remission of our sins. So Paul in 1 Cor. 11:25, 26, interprets these words as referring, not to an oblation but to a partaking of Christ's body and blood: "This do ye, as oft as ye drink it, in remembrance of Me. For as often as ye eat this bread and drink this cup, ye do show the Lord's death till He come." Evidently,

[293] Rev. 14:13.

[294] Cf. John 3:18.

then, Christ's words contain not a single syllable in support of the papistic Mass as a sacrifice for the living and the dead.

Now I again exhort my readers: both in their private deliberations on this question and in their arguments with opponents, they should direct their eyes and their hearts to the words with which the Supper was instituted and which have come down to us from Christ; they should lean upon them, and they should not allow themselves to be turned aside or drawn away from them by any πιθανολογία [persuasive argumentation].[295] For even if the opposition were to cite all the ecclesiastical writers and fathers in confirmation of their view of the Mass, yet believers discern that the express words of our Lord Jesus Christ, the Son of God, must be preferred to all the opinions of men. To this end we should make use of Cyprian's statements in the third epistle of his second book:[296] "If we ought to hear Christ alone, as the eternal[297] Father testifies from heaven, saying, 'This is My well-beloved Son, in whom I am well pleased; hear ye Him,' we ought not to attend to what another before us has thought should be done, but what Christ, who is before all, first did. For it is fitting to follow, not the customs of men but the truth of God."

The Second Argument (which is the most specious of all). "The Catholic Church is the pillar and ground of the truth;[298]

---

[295] See above, note 283, and the text sentence corresponding (which is here repeated almost verbatim).

[296] This quotation is from Cyprian's epistle "to Caecilius, on the Sacrament of the Lord's Cup." It is designated ii. 3. in Manutius' edition, but modern scholars ordinarily number it 63, following Pamelius, the Benedictines, and the Oxford edition. The translation we have given above relies heavily on that by H. Carey in "A Library of Fathers of the Holy Catholic Church, Anterior to the Division of the East and West," ed. Pusey, Keble, Newman, and Marriott (*The Epistles of S. Cyprian, . . . to Which Are Added the Extant Works of S. Pacian* [Oxford: John Henry Parker, 1844], p. 191). The Latin text is available in J.-P. Migne, ed., *Patrologiae cursus completus . . . series Latina,* IV (Paris, 1891), cols. 396, 397, where this casuistical note is quoted from Étienne Baluze (1630—1718): "Ad locum autem istum Cypriani, ubi dicit solum Christum audiendum esse, Joannes cardinalis de Turrecremata [Juan Cardinal de Torquemada (1388—1468)] ait vocem *solus* non excludere papam vel praelatos vel alios doctores aut praedicatores bonos, sed tantum Antichristos, id est contrarios Christo, qui contraria praedicant."

[297] Chytraeus adds "eternal."

[298] Cf. 1 Tim. 3:15.

it could not over so many centuries retain errors and idolatrous ideas in its understanding of the Lord's Supper. Moreover, the Catholic Church as a whole, and all the fathers even from as far back as apostolic times — Ignatius, Irenaeus, Cyprian, Ambrose, Chrysostom, Theophylact,[299] and others — assert positively that the Mass is a sacrifice in which Christ is offered to God the Father and that it should be celebrated even if no communicants are present. Therefore the papists make no mistake but are correct when they teach that the Mass is a sacrifice in which a priest offers God's Son to His eternal Father and by this oblation merits the remission of sins and other benefits for the one performing it and for those to whom it is applied — whether they are among the living, or among the dead in purgatory."

I reply first to the major premise. That the church does not err and is the pillar and ground of the truth, applies not to that church which arrogates to itself the title of true church on the basis of size or regular succession but to that church which is such in fact as well as in name. The true church, in other words, is that body which embraces the pure doctrine of the Gospel and does not defend errors and vanities manifestly repugnant to the Gospel. Compare the situation in Christ's time, when the unbelieving high priests,[300] Sadducees, and Pharisees, who taught that men earned the remission of sins by their own sacrifices, arrogated to themselves the title of God's true church, though they were not; the true church consisted of Zacharias, Simeon, Joseph, Elizabeth, Mary, the shepherds, etc., who kept the true doctrine of Christ[301] and rejected the Pharisaic superstitions and idolatries.

God always preserves among human kind some such company as the latter, but it suffers oppression from the tyranny of hypocrites. And in this little company itself, though most are true believers, some have more light than others and some expound dogma more clearly and accurately than others. Therefore a single absolute and unchangeable norm of truth must be maintained,

[299] See below, note 304.

[300] The Lat. *pontifices* can mean either "high priests" or "popes."

[301] Cf. Luke 2:19, 51; and see Philip Melanchthon, *Loci theologici recogniti* (Leipzig: Officina Voegeliana [1543]), p. 347.

namely, God's Word, by which — as by a Lydian stone — we may test all the beliefs and writings of men.[302]

So even if some testimonies from authoritative writers are marshaled affirming that the Mass is a sacrifice which, applied to the living or the dead, confers the remission of sins and other benefits, it is certain that the word and institution of the one and only Christ ought to be preferred to all the decrees of all the popes and councils.[303] But in fact there were no church Masses without communicants for more than four hundred years after the time of the apostles, and it was during this period that all the fathers lived (with the single exception of Theophylact)[304] whose names appear above in the minor premise. Private Masses for individual priests were first instituted in the Latin Church at the time of Gregory the Great.[305] And no such Masses are said among the Greeks even

---

[302] Lydian stone, or lydite, or Basanite, is a velvet-black flinty jasper which is used as a touchstone for testing the purity of precious metals by their streak. Cf. the Introduction to *The Formula of Concord* (Epitome): "We believe, teach, and confess that the prophetic and apostolic writings of the Old and New Testaments are the only rule and norm according to which all doctrines and teachers alike must be appraised and judged. . . . Holy Scripture remains the only judge, rule, and norm according to which as the only touchstone {*ad Lydium lapidem*} all doctrines should and must be understood and judged as good or evil, right or wrong."

[303] Cf. note 281.

[304] Theophylact, who was born about the middle of the 11th century and died ca. 1110, is remembered chiefly for his exegetical labors; his commentaries on the Minor Prophets, Gospels, Acts, and Pauline epistles, though based on those of Chrysostom, have considerable independent worth.

[305] "Georgii Magni" should read "Gregorii Magni"; the translation has been corrected accordingly. The date of origin of private Masses cannot be determined precisely. Undoubtedly they preceded Gregory (pope 590 to 604) and the later *Gregorian Sacramentary* attributed to him. But it is difficult to prove that they occurred to any appreciable extent during the first "four hundred years after the time of the apostles." Chytraeus' mention of Gregory may connect with the fact that the *Gregorian Sacramentary* came into wide use during the reign of Charlemagne, and this same period is marked by a great increase in the number of private Masses. The following remarks by the Jesuit scholar Braun are of interest in this connection: "Über die Entwicklung der Privatmesse liegt nur ungenügendes Material vor. Immerhin kann kaum ein Zweifel sein, dass neben den Anniversarien, die zu den ältesten missae privatae gehören und in die erste Zeit der jungen

to the present day.[306] Thus one finds it completely impossible to turn the authority of the ancient fathers to the support of the papist argument.

It is true that the fathers call the Lord's Supper a sacrifice, but they themselves explain that they mean, not that Christ's body and blood are offered to God by a priest so as to apply the remission of sins to the living and the dead, but that the rite reminds us of the sacrifice of Christ offered once for all on the altar of the cross. We have pointed out a little earlier that this rite per se cannot rightly be termed a sacrifice. It is not the action of the priest alone but the entire activity of priest and people (viz., commemoration of the death of Christ and all His benefits; faith; prayer; thanksgiving; alms) which the fathers call a sacrifice and oblation.

Indeed, in the Lord's Supper the essence of the Gospel[307] is proclaimed — that Christ was delivered unto death in our behalf, and His own blood was shed for the remission of our sins. Prayers and public thanksgiving for all Christ's benefits accompany this proclamation — this commemoration — of the death and benefits of Christ; a faith on our part is required which does not doubt that because Christ died for us sins have been remitted; a partaking of the body and blood of the Lord is necessary if we would confess and strengthen our faith; and needed also is the sincere intention to maintain this faith and obey God. In the early church each communicant brought oblations of money, bread, wine, vegetables,

Kirche hinaufreichen, bereits in der zweiten Hälfte des 5. Jahrhunderts auch sonstige Privatmessen recht häufig gewesen sein werden. . . . So gebräuchlich waren in der Karolingerzeit die Privatmessen geworden, dass manche Priester sich keineswegs täglich mit einer Messe begnügten, sondern zwei, drei, ja mehr derselben an demselben Tage lasen." (Joseph Braun, Der christliche Altar in seiner geschichtlichen Entwicklung, I [Munich: Koch, [1924], 375, 376.) Probably Chytraeus here relies on the Augsburg Confession, XXIV, 35 (Latin).

306 This is correct. The missa privata is a form of Low Mass, and "the Orthodox have no provision for Low Mass. . . . As they only celebrate on Sundays and feast-days, they have less need for any service like our Low Mass" (Adrian Fortescue, The Orthodox Eastern Church [London: Catholic Truth Society, 1916], p. 418, n. 2).

307 A misprint of Enangelii for Euangelii appears in the text at this point.

and fruit, which they presented following the chanting of the Creed;[308] some of the loaves and part of the wine were consecrated, and afterwards the rest was customarily distributed to the poor and to the clergy for their use.[309]

All of these things taken together the fathers call an oblation and a sacrifice, that is to say, a eucharistic offering — and so they term the Lord's Supper a εὐχαριστία [Eucharist]. As Irenaeus says of this New Testament sacrifice, "We must make our oblation to God and in all things be found grateful to God the Creator, with a pure mind and faith without hypocrisy, with firm hope, with fervent love offering the firstfruits of His own creatures; and this oblation the church alone offers pure to the Creator, presenting it to Him with thanksgiving from His creation."[310]

Now even though we were to concede that the fathers believed that the Lord's Supper or Mass was a sacrifice in which Christ is offered to God, there are many more things in the conclusion of the above argument than can be deduced from its premises. For it does not follow that this oblation earns the remission of sins for the living and release from the pains of purgatory for the dead, or that these benefits are through the Mass applied *ex opere*

---

[308] "Anciently the minister intoned the opening phrase, 'I believe in God,' and the choir and congregation continued with 'the Father Almighty.' . . . Luther in his German Mass prepared a versification of the Creed to be sung by congregations. At the present time we are so accustomed to saying the Creed that the singing of it might seem strange. There is much to be said for this, however, where proper leadership is available." (Luther D. Reed, *The Lutheran Liturgy* [Philadelphia: Muhlenberg Press, 1947], p. 287.) In Chytraeus' day the Creed was normally chanted; cf. the Marburg Articles, I (closing words).

[309] "During the first two centuries Christian worship was essentially congregational. . . . The congregation was a universal priesthood. Under the direction of recognized leaders, it offered its spiritual sacrifices of prayer, praise, and thanksgiving and brought its gifts of bread and wine for the Eucharist and for distribution to the poor." (Ibid., p. 31; cf. Reed, *Worship: A Study of Corporate Devotion* [Philadelphia: Muhlenberg Press, 1959], p. 4)

[310] Irenaeus, *Adversus haereses*, IV. xviii. 4; original (Lat.) text in J.-P. Migne, ed., *Patrologiae cursus completus . . . series Graeca*, VII (Paris, 1857), cols. 1026—27. The English translation given above is based on that in Henry Bettenson, ed., *Documents of the Christian Church* (New York and London: Oxford University Press, 1950), p. 104.

131

operato[311] to others, etc. It is evident from the writings of the fathers that they never dreamed of such monstrous notions.[312]

The Third Argument. "In every period of the world's history — even as far back as Abel — the church has had a definite priesthood and a definite, visible sacrifice (like the perennial sacrifice,[313] etc., commanded by the Law) which this priesthood has the responsibility of offering. Therefore, today as well there must be a priesthood in the church, and for that priesthood a definite, visible sacrifice — specifically, the sacrifice of the Mass, which was received from the apostles, as Irenaeus testifies, and which the church has preserved continuously for fifteen hundred years, even to the present time."

I reply by rejecting the conclusion. I do this, first, because in the Old Testament the external sacrificial rites were shadows or types of things which were to be revealed in the New Testament. Heb. 10:1: "The Law has a shadow of good things to come, and not the very image of the things," i. e., not the real and final thing. Col. 2:17: "These are a shadow of things to come, but the body is of Christ." Hence it follows that under the New Covenant we ought to seek the real things, that is, the sacrifices which those Old Testament types represent, rather than external ceremonies similar to the ones in the Old Testament. The sacrificial rites of the Law point especially to Christ's sacrifice, in which on the altar of the cross He offered Himself *once* to His eternal Father to cancel out sin. Because of this the New Covenant has no other visible

311 See above, note 240.

312 Although this may seem to be an exaggerated assertion on our author's part, the similar — and unrefuted — claim of his contemporary John Jewel puts the statement in a somewhat different light. In 1559 and 1560, Jewel, an Englishman and one of the greatest patristic scholars of his time, challenged all comers to prove by the fathers the Romanist-sacrificial doctrine of the Eucharist. He baldly stated: "If any learned man alive were able to prove [such] . . . by any one clear or plain sentence of the scriptures, or of the old doctors, or of any old general council, or by any example of the primitive church, for the space of six hundred years after Christ, he would give over and subscribe unto him" (John Jewel, *Works* [Parker Society edition], I, 20, 21; quoted in the provocative article by Geoffrey W. Bromiley, "Who Are the True Catholics?" in *Christianity Today,* IV [Oct. 26, 1959], 11, 12).

313 See above, section II. A. 1.

sacrifice which merits the remission of sins or is able to be applied to others. Nor does the New Testament contain any ceremonial sacrifice of a eucharistic kind which priests or others can offer to God; instead, all Christians alike — clergy and laity — are to offer up spiritual sacrifices under the illumination provided by a knowledge of Christ and faith in Him, and these oblations consist of prayer, thanksgiving, confession, patience, and full Christian obedience (1 Peter 2:5).

My second point relates to the views of Irenaeus, who writes in Bk. IV, chap. 32:[314] "Christ taught a new oblation of the New Testament,[315] which the church, receiving from the apostles, offers to God throughout the world, even to Him who gives us nourishment, as the firstfruits of His own gifts in the New Testament, concerning which Malachi spoke beforehand in the Twelve Prophets...." It is clear to one who reads the whole section (chapters 32 and 33)[316] that what Irenaeus calls the oblation of the New Testament is not a sacrifice of Christ's body and blood at the Supper (we have shown previously that such a sacrifice contradicts almost every letter [317] of the Verba), but the entire cultus of the New Testament: genuine knowledge of God, faith, thanksgiving, confession of faith through partaking of Christ's body and blood, new obedience, and particularly the alms, bread, wine, vegetables, and fruit, which, after the chanting of the Creed, the people used to offer at the table of the Lord for the benefit of the poor and the clergy.[318] These gifts Irenaeus describes as "the oblations of firstfruits from God's creatures." [319] It was from these offerings at the altar that the Lord's Supper first came to be designated a sacrifice.

Third, even if Irenaeus had spoken of a sacrifice of the body

---

[314] Chytraeus refers to Irenaeus' *Adv. haereses;* in terms of the chapter divisions now used, the passage appears in IV. xvii. 5 (Migne, *Patrologiae cursus completus . . . series Graeca,* VII, col. 1023). Our English translation follows F. R. M. Hitchcock, *The Treatise of Irenaeus of Lugdunum Against the Heresies: A Translation of the Principal Passages, with Notes and Arguments,* II (London: S. P. C. K., 1916), 36.

[315] *Testementi* occurs as a misprint for *Testamenti* here.

[316] In modern numeration, *Adv. haer.* IV. xvii. 1—6.

[317] See above, note 286 and the text corresponding.

[318] See notes 308, 309.

[319] See the text corresponding to note 310.

and blood of God's Son at the Supper, one cannot deduce from it the monstrous idea that that oblation earns the remission of sins *ex opere operato* [320] for the one performing it and for others, whether living or dead, to whom it is applied. But to assume that Irenaeus is talking about a sacrifice of Christ's body and blood is quite false and violates his context, as appears from his words "we offer the firstfruits of God's creatures" — for the Son of God is no creature!

In the fourth place,[321] whatever Irenaeus' view was, let us "not attend to something a man before us has said or written, but what Christ, who is before all, said and did," [322] and let us forever keep before our eyes, as the sole norm of truth, the words of institution used at the Lord's Supper, which say nothing of oblation or of application on behalf of others but only of partaking and of receiving by faith the remission of our sins.

* * *

Here ends our detailed exposition of the principal topics comprising the doctrine of priesthood and sacrifice in the Old and New Testaments.

[320] See above, note 240.

[321] The text should read *quarto* instead of *quinto*. This point is designated *quinto* in the *Commentary on Matthew,* which is being followed here (see above, note 284); although for the *De sacrificiis* our author altered the numeration of the other points, he neglected to make the corresponding alteration in the number of this final point.

[322] Chytraeus again uses a patristic authority (Cyprian) to counter the Romanists who appeal to patristic authority; for the quotation, see note 296 and the corresponding text.

WORKS CITED BY ABBREVIATIONS
IN THE NOTES

A-G   Bauer, Walter. *A Greek-English Lexicon of the New Testament and Other Early Christian Literature.* Trans. and adapted from Bauer's *Griechisch-Deutsches Wörterbuch,* 4th ed., by W. F. Arndt and F. W. Gingrich. Chicago: University of Chicago Press; Cambridge: Cambridge University Press, 1957.

All-Gren   Allen, J. H., and Greenough, J. B. *New Latin Grammar . . . Founded on Comparative Grammar.* Rev. ed. Ed. by G. L. Kittredge, *et al.* Boston: Ginn and Company, 1903.

B-J   Baxter, J. H., and Johnson, Charles. *Medieval Latin Word-List.* Prepared under the Direction of a Committee Appointed by the British Academy. London: Oxford University Press, 1934.

BDB   Gesenius, Wilhelm. *A Hebrew and English Lexicon of the Old Testament.* Trans. and adapted from Gesenius' *Lexicon Manuale* by Edward Robinson. Ed. with additions by Francis Brown, S. R. Driver, and C. A. Briggs. Oxford: Clarendon Press, 1952.

D-B   Deferrari, R. J., and Barry, Sister M. Inviolata. *A Lexicon of St. Thomas Aquinas.* Washington, D. C.: Catholic University of America Press, 1948—49. 5 fascs.

EG   Nicoll, W. R., ed. *The Expositor's Greek Testament.* Reprint ed. Grand Rapids: Eerdmans, 1951. 5 vols.

G-G   Goodwin, W. W. *Greek Grammar.* Rev. by C. B. Gulick. Boston: Ginn and Company, 1930.

K   Kittel, Rudolf, ed. *Biblia Hebraica.* Rev. by A. Alt and O. Eissfeldt. 7th ed. Stuttgart: Privileg. Württembergische Bibelanstalt, 1951.

L-S   Liddell, H. G., and Scott, Robert. *A Greek-English Lexicon.* Rev. by H. S. Jones and Roderick McKenzie. Oxford: Clarendon Press, 1925—40. 2 vols.

OCD   *The Oxford Classical Dictionary.* Ed. by M. Cary, *et al.* Oxford: Clarendon Press, 1949.

R   Rahlfs, Alfred, ed. *Septuaginta.* 4th ed. Stuttgart: Privileg. Württembergische Bibelanstalt, 1950. 2 vols.

SGLL   Souter, Alexander. *A Glossary of Later Latin to 600 A. D.* Oxford: Clarendon Press, 1949.

SUBSTANTIVE VARIATA IN THE 1599 EDITION
OF THE *DE SACRIFICIIS*

[a] *Omit* "doctrine of the priesthood and"

[b] *Omit* "priesthood and"

[c] *Add* "of which some portion was separated out for the priests and for a communal feast"

[d] *Omit* "priestly"

[e] *Add* "or 'worshiping God' "

[f] *Add* "or sacred function" (*sacrum officium*)

[g] *For* "Lev. 6" *read* "Lev. 16"

[h] *Omit* "to be"

[i] *For* "appears in Hebrew as" *read* "Heb. 13;"

[j] *For* "Ex. 13, 23; Lev. 2, 23; Deut. 26" *read* "Ex. 13, 22, 34; Lev. 2, 23; Num. 18; Deut. 12, 15, 18, 26" *Omit* the last sentence (point 6) in this paragraph.

[k] *Add* "Deut. 18"

[l] *Invert the order of* points 3 and 4

[m] *For* "for" *read* "by means of"

[n] *For* "fear" *read* "be bound by"

[o] *Add* "Here ends our account of the kinds of sacrifices."

[p] *Omit* "may"

[q] *Omit* "had"

[r] *Add* explicit numeration of this series

[s] *For* "All these" *read* "Here all the"

[t] *Add* "their own good works"

[u] *Add* "10, and"

[v] *Add* ", ex opere operato"

[w] *Add* "Mark 12:32, 33."

[x] *Omit* rubric

[y] *For* ", i. e., the Law and the Gospel of Christ" *read* "to the church"

[z] *For* "granted" *read* "intrusted"

[aa] *Add* as marginal rubric "Spiritual Sacrifices Common to All Christians"

[bb] *Add* the following lines of Christian hymnody/poetry:

> Spirituale mihi constructum in pectore templum est,
> Incrustatum agni sanguine ubique Dei.
> Hic pater, hic gnatus, simul hic spirabile numen,

Sancta trias sedem gaudet habere suam.
Parva quidem domus est, sed in hac habitantibus illis,
Ampla sat, et vere est regia tota domus.
Hanc precor, hanc sedem, Deus hoc habitato sacellum,
Hancque tuam labi ne patiare domum.

cc *Omit* "even"

dd *Omit* this sentence

ee *Italicize* (for emphasis) the first two sentences of this paragraph

ff *For* "Reims" *read* "Sens" *Add* "in Spain, Toledo; in England, Canterbury; in Hungary, Esztergom;"

gg *Omit* "wicked"

hh *Add* "μεταμορφοῦσθε" (Gk. for "be ye transformed" in Rom. 12:2)

ii *Add* as marginal rubric "Kinds" *(Species)* [of spiritual sacrifices]

jj *Add* as marginal rubric "Efficient Cause" [of spiritual sacrifices]

kk *Add* as marginal rubric "Formal Cause, or How May the Sacrifices Please God?"

ll *Add* as marginal rubric "Purposes of the Sacrifices"

mm *Omit* "at length"

nn *For* "the words . . . his Gospel." *read* "the theological topic of the Sacraments — Baptism and the Eucharist." [Chytraeus discusses Baptism at the very end of his *Commentary on Matthew* (pp. 708—57 of the 1575 ed.), and both subjects are dealt with in his *De Baptismo et Eucharistia, ex praelectionibus Davidis Chytraei excepta,* ed. Zachary Lemann (Wittenberg, 1584).]

oo The 1599 ed. of the *De Sacrificiis* terminates at this point.

APPENDIX

A SHORT CRITIQUE
OF GUSTAF AULÉN'S *CHRISTUS VICTOR*

*Evaluation of the Three Atonement Theories
as Characterized by Aulén*

In order to offer the clearest possible picture of Aulén's argument in *Christus Victor,* we present the following tabular schema of the three atonement theories with which he deals. It should be emphasized that the data given in the table represent Aulén's descriptions of these atonement theories[1] and that these descriptions are not necessarily accepted as factually accurate or complete by the present author.

"Classic" theory (Fathers, Luther)	*"Latin doctrine"* (Anselm, Lutheran Orthodoxy)	*"Subjective"* view (Abelard, Schleiermacher, Ritschl)
1. Continuity of divine operation	1. Discontinuity of divine operation	1. Human operation (conversion or amendment)
a. Atonement planned by God	a. Atonement planned by God	a. No consistent stand taken on the source of the "atonement" plan
b. Accomplished by God in the person of Christ	b. Accomplished by Christ as sinless Man suffering God's wrath against sins of the world	b. Accomplished by Jesus as exemplary Man
c. God approaches (▼) man	c. Man approaches (▲) God	c. Man approaches (▲) God

[1] The data in the table are derived principally from pp. 145—158 of *Christus Victor: An Historical Study of the Three Main Types of the Idea of the Atonement,* trans. A. G. Hebert (New York: Macmillan, 1956). The reader is referred to this section for detailed explanations of assertions in the table. Helpful collateral reading may be found in Aulén's *Faith of the Christian Church,* trans. E. H. Wahlstrom and G. E. Arden (Philadelphia: Muhlenberg Press, 1948), pp. 223—241, and in Nels F. S. Ferré's *Swedish Contributions to Modern Theology, with Special Reference to Lundensian Thought* (New York: Harper, 1939), pp. 153—165 ("The Religious View of the Atonement"). Bishop Aulén himself, incidentally, read portions of Ferré's manuscript and offered suggestions on it before its publication.

d. Incarnation and atonement closely related	d. Incarnation separated from atonement	d. Neither incarnation nor atonement stressed; Jesus the Pattern Man
e. Atonement, justification, sanctification seen as different aspects of virtually the same thing	e. Atonement, justification seen as successive, separate operations	e. Sanctification stressed, with atonement and justification playing little part
2. Discontinuity of merit and justice; grace and love stressed	2. Continuity of merit and justice; Law stressed	2. Neither justice nor grace receive much emphasis; human love stressed
3. Dualistic emphasis — ransom paid to the devil (yet God all-sovereign)	3. Monistic emphasis — ransom paid to God	3. Monistic emphasis — devil not regarded with much seriousness
a. The sinner freed from the power of sin, death, devil	a. Christ's merits imputed to the sinner	a. Man given a new motive for obedience
b. Sin, death, devil all stressed as powers to be dealt with	b. Sin stressed as the power to be dealt with	b. Little stress on evil power
c. Triumphal, positive emphasis	c. Negative emphasis (man's penalty legally removed)	c. Optimistic emphasis
4. Paradoxical tensions maintained	4. Attempt at rational construction	4. Attempt at rational construction

What light will an examination of Scripture shed on the truth value of these three atonement doctrines? Let us consider in turn each of the four main characteristics of these theories: (1) In a larger sense, *sub specie aeternitatis*, the atonement was surely a continuous work of God, as the "classic" doctrine asserts. Acts 2:22, 23: "Jesus of Nazareth . . . being delivered by the determinate counsel and foreknowledge of God, ye have taken and by wicked hands have crucified." John 6:38: "I [Christ] came down from heaven, not to do Mine own will but the will of Him that sent Me." Luke 22:42: "Father, if Thou be willing, remove this cup from Me; nevertheless not My will but Thine be done."

However, in a more narrow (but no less real) sense, Scripture presents a sharp discontinuity which reaches its climax in the agonized words of Christ on the cross: ὁ θεός μου ὁ θεός μου, εἰς τί ἐγκατέλιπές με; Christ did in fact, as man, suffer the full effect of God's wrath directed against the sins of the world. 2 Cor. 5:21: "For our sake He [God] made Him [Christ] to be sin who knew no sin, so that in Him we might become the righteousness of God." 1 Peter 3:18: "Christ also hath once suffered for sins, the Just for the unjust, that He might bring us to God." Gal. 3:13: "Christ hath redeemed us from the curse of the Law, being made a curse for us." There is perhaps no clearer doctrine expressed in Scripture than Paul's delineation of Christ as the "Second Adam" — as the Representative Man who reconciled the race to God. 1 Cor. 15:45: "The first man, Adam, was made a living soul; the last Adam was made a quickening spirit." Rom. 5:15: "If through the offense of one many be dead, much more the grace of God, and the gift by grace, which is by one Man, Jesus Christ, hath abounded unto many." In this (admittedly secondary) sense, man did approach God in the atonement. Moreover, though incarnation, atonement, justification, and sanctification are generally presented in Scripture as mere aspects of a single great plan, the very fact that separate words such as δικαίωσις and ἁγιασμός are employed indicates that these concepts are sometimes thought of as separate, discrete operations (cf. Rom. 8:30).

And when we consider the "subjective" doctrine, we find not merely the inadequacies which Aulén sees in it but definite Scriptural merits as well. Charles M. Sheldon (*In His Steps*) has shown beyond a doubt the power in that Scriptural text which reads: "Christ also suffered for us, leaving us an example, that ye should follow His steps" (1 Peter 2:21). The "subjective" view rightly sees that Jesus' work on the cross is of no value to an individual or a society without repentance and faith. Luke 13:3: "I tell you . . . Except ye repent, ye shall all likewise perish." Acts 16:31: πίστευσον ἐπὶ τὸν κύριον Ἰησοῦν, καὶ σωθήσῃ σύ.[2] Finally, the "subjective" theory places an emphasis on sanctification which is very Scriptural and very healthy. 1 Thess. 4:3: "This is the will of God, even your sanctification." James 2:26: "Faith without works is dead."

It thus becomes evident that with regard to point (1) each of the atonement theories as presented by Aulén has definite values not possessed by the others. Conversely, each lacks emphases which are Scriptural and vital — for the "classic" view does not sufficiently stress Christ as Representative Man offering Himself to God for the sins of the world; the "Latin doctrine" myopically fails to see the all-over continuity of the divine redemptive plan; and the "subjective" view, as the word "subjective" indicates, superficially misses the objective and profoundly efficacious character of the atonement as it is presented in Holy Writ.

(2) As in the preceding case, the atonement doctrine which Aulén terms "classic" presents the more ultimate Scriptural truth: Grace and love did in fact triumph over law and justice on the cross. The words of Hugh of St. Victor cross the centuries with undiminished power: "Non quia reconciliavit amavit, sed quia amavit reconciliavit."[3] But this is hardly the whole story. Law and

---

[2] Note the aorist imperative and future passive indicative. Both the aorist and future tenses have punctiliar *Aktionsart,* and the indicative in the apodosis of this implied condition carries with it a feeling of great certainty and definiteness.

[3] Quoted on the title page of George Cadwalader Foley, *Anselm's Theory of the Atonement* (New York: Longmans, 1909).

justice had profound roles to play in the drama whose last act (or rather, next-to-last act!) was played out on Golgotha. Christ did act as a substitute for sinful mankind, as we have already pointed out (2 Cor. 5:21; 1 Peter 3:18; Gal. 3:13). He fulfilled the demands of the Law and then died so that those who had broken the Law might not have to die. Unless substitutionary, "legalistic" (if you will) sacrifice is retained as an element in the atonement, the New Testament book of Hebrews becomes meaningless, and the vital connection between the Old Testament sacrificial system and the perfect sacrifice of Christ in the New Testament is lost. One who doubts the deep significance of the "Latin doctrine" in this regard need only read James Denney's *Death of Christ*.[4] The "subjective" doctrine again stresses the necessity of human response to the act of God in Christ, but needless to say, it runs the risk of perverting the total atonement picture, because Law and grace are not emphasized as well.

(3) When we come to matters of dualism-monism, we find Scripturally that the "Latin doctrine," rather than the "classic" theory, provides the more ultimate interpretation. The existence of a personal devil and a host of evil forces is clearly asserted in Scripture (temptation of Christ passages; Eph. 6:12), but these powers of darkness are never viewed as eternal opposites to God, as was Ahriman in Zoroastrianism. The evil forces in the universe exist only because God permits it; here the opening chapters of the Old Testament book of Job can be consulted profitably and compared with New Testament passages such as Col. 1:16. Thus, even though some of the fathers do say that Christ paid His ransom to the devil, yet in a more fundamental sense the ransom was paid to God (Heb. 9:14), who, in His *opus alienum,* allowed the evil powers to gain a certain legitimate sway over sinful mankind.

The "classic" view rightly stresses the unholy triad of evil influences — sin, death, and the devil; and not to do so is to restrict the scope of the Biblical plan of salvation (Heb. 2:14-17). On the other hand the "Latin doctrine" is very correct in centering attention on the sin factor, for unless this is done, one's conception of the atonement becomes grossly "physical" (where death is emphasized), or the vital issue of personal human responsibility for sin becomes neglected (where satanic activity is stressed). The triumphal, positive mood of the "classic" theory is of course thoroughly Biblical and is illustrated in such magnificent New Testament passages as Rom. 8:37-39; 1 Cor. 15; and Rev. 20 and 21.

(4) The "classic" theory sees deeply into Scriptural doctrine when it makes no attempt rationally to resolve the paradoxical character of the

---

[4] E. g., as edited by Prof. R. V. G. Tasker of the University of London (Chicago: Inter-Varsity Christian Fellowship, 1952). Cf. Eugene R. Fairweather, "Incarnation and Atonement: An Anselmian Response to Aulén's *Christus Victor,*" *Canadian Journal of Theology,* VII (July 1961), 167—175.

atonement. Isaiah, shortly after giving us his great "substitution" chapter (Is. 53), utters one of the profoundest sentences in all of Scripture: לֹא מַחְשְׁבוֹתַי מַחְשְׁבוֹתֵיכֶם וְלֹא דַרְכֵיכֶם דְּרָכָי נְאֻם יְהוָה׃ (Is. 55:8). And yet (existentialism notwithstanding) paradoxes are not to be made more severe than Scripture makes them. There is no utility in a contradiction *qua* contradiction. The "credo quia absurdum" type of theology is repugnant not only to the serious believer but also to the inquiring unbeliever. Both the "substitutionary" and the "new motive" rationales for the atonement are clearly present in Holy Writ, as we have attempted to show, though they are not intended to remove the ultimate "offense of the cross" (1 Cor. 1:22-25). In explaining the atonement to the Galatians by means of legal analogy, Paul clearly states the limitations of his explanation, but the fact that limitations necessarily exist does not prevent him (as it does many moderns) from giving any explanation at all. Paul writes: "Brethren, I speak after the manner of men: though it be but a man's covenant, yet if it be confirmed, no man disannulleth or addeth thereto" (Gal. 3:15; note the context of this verse). The "Latin doctrine" and the "subjective" view do not become unbiblical simply because they attempt to understand the atonement; they do, however, lose their right to speak authoritatively when they assert or imply that their rational explanations constitute the total picture. Any "explanation" of kerygmatic doctrine must always, by the nature of the case, "speak after the manner of men."

Aulén's Cross-Division
The Crucial Difficulty in Lundensian Theology

The preceding discussion has made rather clear that Aulén's partiality for what he calls the "classic" atonement doctrine is not fully justified on Scriptural grounds. On issues (1), (2), and (4) the "classic" doctrine states the more ultimate truth — *sub specie aeternitatis;* but this does not mean that the emphases of the other two theories on these very issues do not have Scriptural sanction. On the monism-dualism problem we have in the "Latin doctrine" (and to a lesser extent in the "subjective" view) a more fundamental Biblical viewpoint presented than that given by the "classic" theory; yet on this issue as well, the "classic" view offers healthy insights. The point we wish to make is that no one of the three theories delineated by Aulén contains the whole Biblical picture of the atoning work of Christ.

Now since our author is more interested in the truth value of atonement theories than in the bare historical presentation of them, we have in *Christus Victor* a patent case of what the logicians, taxonomists, and library classifiers term "cross-division" or "cross-classification." Let us hear L. S. Stebbing on the theory of classification:[5]

The basis of division (i. e., the differentiating characteristics) is

[5] L. Susan Stebbing, *A Modern Introduction to Logic* (London: Methuen, 1930), p. 435.

often called by the Latin name *"fundamentum divisionis."* The principles regulating a logical division are usually summed up in the following rules:

1. There must be only one *fundamentum divisionis* at each step.
2. The division must be exhaustive.
3. The successive steps of the division (if there be more than one) must proceed by gradual stages.

From Rule 1 there follows the corollary that the classes must be mutually exclusive. Violation of this rule results in the fallacy of *cross-division,* or overlapping classes. For example, if *vehicles* were divided into *public vehicles, private vehicles, motor-cars* and *lorries,* there would be more than one basis of division, with the result that the classes would overlap.

Bishop Aulén has inadvertently allowed himself two *fundamenta divisionis* at his first step of classification — the *fundamentum* of theological truth and the *fundamentum* of historical coherence. In attempting two things at once, he has really succeeded in neither. As we have said, we are concerned more chiefly with the truth-value issue, but it is well to note in passing that purely from a historical standpoint the three atonement views given by our author cannot be considered as distinct as he would have us believe. Luther did not present solely "classic" ideas of the atonement,[6] nor was Anselm entirely free from "classic" influences in *Cur Deus Homo;*[7] and the same could be said for practically all other writers on the atonement through Christian history. The reason for this is obvious: the ultimate source of atonement doctrine is Holy Writ, and Holy Writ is not exclusively "classic," "Latin," or "subjective" in its view of Christ's work on the cross.

Since he is primarily interested in the truth value of atonement theories, our author should certainly have used "Scriptural soundness" and "Scriptural unsoundness" as his two main genera of classification, and then (if he wished) various "historical types" of atonement theory as species under each of these

---

[6] Read, for example, Luther's exposition of Ps. 51:7 (in *Luther's Works,* ed. Jaroslav Pelikan, XII [St. Louis: Concordia, 1955], 359—367). In this exposition both "Latin" and "subjective" elements are clearly present.

[7] Note, e. g., Bk. I, chaps. 5 and 6, whose titles are respectively: "How the redemption of man could not be effected by any other being but God"; "How infidels find fault with us for saying that God has redeemed us by his death, and thus has shown his love toward us, and that he came to overcome the devil for us" (St. Anselm, *Cur Deus Homo?,* trans. Sidney Norton Deane [Chicago: Open Court, 1903], pp. 184 to 186). Walter Marshall Horton is of course correct when he says *(Our Eternal Contemporary)* that Aulén considers the "classic" atonement view to be more inclusive than the others, rather than completely distinct from them; yet in the last analysis *Christus Victor* is Aulén's attempt to separate the "classic" theory from the two theories which have held the field in the past and to place the "classic" view on a par with them — treating it as the "genuine, authentic Christian faith" (p. 159).

two genera. Yet he did not do this; in fact, no thorough Biblical analysis of atonement theories appears in *Christus Victor*. There is no chapter at all devoted to the "Old Testament," and the "New Testament" chapter appears — and this is very significant when we consider Aulén's attitude toward patristics — *after* a chapter on "Irenaeus" and one on "the Fathers in East and West." At this point we begin to grasp a basic problem both in Aulén's theological approach and in that of the Lundensian theology of which he has been a prime spokesman.[8]

Aulén's blunder of "cross-division" is due to the lack of a clear-cut Biblical standard of theological evaluation — and this same difficulty plagues all of modern Lundensian thought. The Lundensians refuse to employ the historical criterion of conformity to the Christian Scriptures as interpreted by the *analogia fidei*. Anders Nygren writes:[9]

> The reason that historical truths are insufficient as a foundation for faith is their relative degree of certainty. Even the facts most definitely ascertained possess but relative certainty, while the very nature of faith requires absolute certainty for its foundation. . . . Only the a priori has apodictic certainty.

And what is the principal a priori involved in Lundensian thought? It is the concept of *sola gratia* and its motivating force, agape love (as Nygren's *Agape and Eros* clearly states). When one realizes this, it becomes easy to see why Aulén stresses the atonement characteristics he describes as "classic": all four of the "classic" characteristics, as we have listed them above, emphasize God's unmerited grace and love toward His fallen creatures. We should note that the inadequacy of our author's position becomes evident at this very point where its greatest strength lies; for even if we admit (as we in fact do) that agape-motivated grace is the most fundamental and ultimate theological principle, this principle is *not* the whole theological story, and therefore, if it is taken completely by itself, it will inevitably pervert one's conception of the divine plan of salvation.[10]

It was not for nothing that the Reformers employed three great theological principles — not only *sola gratia* but also *sola fide* and *sola Scriptura*. The only effective counteractant to Lundensian one-sidedness is to return to the historical Scriptures (and to the *historical* Christ on whom they center) as the formal

---

[8] "Gustaf Aulén, whose imprint on Lundensian ideology is in certain aspects the heaviest. . . ." (Ferré, op. cit., p. 26)

[9] In *Religiöst apriori*, pp. 15, 16 (quoted by Ferré, op. cit., p. 55).

[10] We are of course acquainted with the fact that the Lundensian school arose "as a reaction to the indefiniteness of a confused liberalism" which manifested "bewildered relativism" (Ferré, op. cit., p. 23). Thus the Lundensian position was itself a healthy counteractant to a far more theologically questionable extreme; yet two wrongs do not make a right, even when considered from the standpoint of Hegel's thesis-antithesis-synthesis dialectic!

principle — the source and norm — of all theological doctrine; [11] and to return to the *sola fide* principle as the means of appropriating the grace of God in individual lives. Had Aulén stressed Scriptural authority more, he would not have passed such a negative verdict on the substitutionary "Latin doctrine" of the atonement; had he stressed the *sola fide* principle more, he would have seen more clearly the profound truth resident in the "subjective" theory, namely, that "without faith it is impossible to please Him."

In conclusion, then, we give credit to our author where credit is due — we praise his insight into the fundamental and vital "classic" aspects of the atonement; but at the same time we plead for a return to the complete Reformation motto of *sola gratia, sola fide, sola Scriptura*. Only when such a return is made will we avoid the theological blunder of pitting good things against each other, and only then will we be willing to accept all the facets of evangelical Christian doctrine.

[11] We should fully realize that, unless the Scriptures are taken as the theological *principium cognoscendi*, Aulén's a priori of *sola gratia* cannot be defended against any other theological a priori (for example, the exact opposite of *sola gratia*, Pelagio-Arminian synergism!).

SCRIPTURE INDEX